ARISTOTLE
AND HIS
MODERN CRITICS

ARISTOTLE
AND HIS
MODERN CRITICS
The Use of Tragedy in the
Nontragic Vision

Patrick Madigan

Scranton: University of Scranton Press
London and Toronto: Associated University Pressses

© 1992 by Associated University Presses, Inc.

Associated University Presses
440 Forsgate Drive
Cranbury, NJ 08512

Associated University Presses
25 Sicilian Avenue
London WC1A 2QH, England

Associated University Presses
P.O. Box 39, Clarkson Pstl. Stn.
Mississauga, Ontario
L5J 3X9 Canada

The paper used in this publication meets the requirements of the American National Standard for Permanence of Paper for Printed Library Materials Z39.48-1984.

Library of Congress Cataloging-in-Publication Data

Madigan, Patrick, 1945–
Aristotle and his modern critics : the use of tragedy in the nontragic vision / Patrick Madigan.
p.   cm.
Includes bibliographical references and index.
ISBN 0-940866-13-7 (alk. paper)
1. Aristotle.   2. Tragedy.   3. Aristotle.   I. Title.
B485.M24   1992
808.2—dc20   90-72044
                              CIP

PRINTED IN THE UNITED STATES OF AMERICA

It is in Greek tragedy that the theme of the man "blinded" and led to his destruction by the gods is carried all at once to the uttermost limit of its virulence, so that thereafter the analogues of Greek tragedy are perhaps only muted expressions of the same *insupportable* revelation. . . . Perhaps the tragic cannot tolerate transcription into a theory which—let us say it immediately—could only be the scandalous theology of predestination to evil. Perhaps the tragic theology must be rejected as soon as it is thought. Perhaps also it is capable of surviving, as spectacle, all the destructions that follow upon its transcription into the plain language of speculation. The connection with a spectacle, then, would be the specific means by which the *symbolic* power that resides in every tragic myth could be protected. At the same time, the connection with a spectacle, with the theater, would have the value of a warning and of an invitation. . . . If, then, the religious consciousness hesitates to *formulate* the tragic theology, that is because elsewhere it professes "the innocence of God," to speak Platonic language, or the "holiness" in Biblical language. Explicit formulation of the tragic theology would mean self-destruction for the religious consciousness.

—Paul Ricoeur
The Symbolism of Evil

What Aristotle sensed was that a tragic hero (if there is one) must engage our sympathies, lest we simply wait for, and at last rejoice in, his destruction. Aristotle further sensed that the utterly gratuitous destruction of a noble and completely innocent character would be less apt to lead to a catharsis than the downfall of a hero who, though noble and admired by us, had done something that led to his fall. What Aristotle failed to see was that a poet of sufficient genius could gain our sympathies even for Richard III and Macbeth, and—much more important, because these two are exceptions—that no flaw or error is required for a noble human being to do something that eventually leads to his or her destruction or some other catastrophe. This last point Aristotle should have recognized because it was the crux of Sophoclean tragedy. . . . Aristotle's reason for attributing some *hamartia* to those who suffer and are destroyed was that he considered totally undeserved suffering shocking rather than tragic. . . . Like Job's friends, (he) imputes moral fault. But a man's destruction may be brought about by his choice, his act, his heroism, though he is morally admirable.

—Walter Kaufmann
Tragedy and Philosophy

Contents

ARISTOTLE
AND HIS
MODERN CRITICS

Introduction

Some of us brought up and educated in what seems today the genteel, prelapsarian 1950s were trained, in neo-Aristotelian fashion, to distinguish the "fine arts" from the "practical arts." The fine arts were those which were done for no end beyond themselves; they were enjoyed for their own sakes, or were values in themselves. The practical arts had an end beyond themselves, were done because of this external value, and were esteemed in function of the end they served and how efficiently they produced it. The fine arts were in a sense superior to the practical arts because the practical arts existed to serve and produce the fine arts, rather than vice versa. This distinction, which begins the *Nicomachean Ethics*, was assumed to apply preeminently to the arts such as painting, drama, and literature although Aristotle never mentions these in this context; he more commonly mentions governance and contemplation. In fact, the distinction does not appear in the *Poetics* at all.

A strange sort of "marriage of convenience" took place in the 1940s and 1950s, when this neo-Aristotelian distinction was fused with, or mapped onto, that phase of late nineteenth-century romanticism, the *fin de siècle* aestheticism called "New Criticism." After the hiatus of two world wars, which were ascribed to the ascendancy of "technological reason," "ideology," "materialism" and the "pragmatic cult of efficiency," this movement joined the world-weariness of T. S. Elliot's attack on modernism with the self-conscious primitivism and irrationalism of Faulkner and the Southern Agrarians, in a violent lashing

11

out against most forms of objective reason, lambasted as the father of Deweyite Instrumentalism, mechanistic scientific materialism, and totalitarianism, to create the aesthetic creed of New Criticism. This was the first time, at least on this side of the Atlantic, that aestheticism was married to a traditional or conservative, as opposed to a liberal or revolutionary, point of view.

This new movement accentuated the contrast between the fine and practical arts beyond Aristotle; in fact, the contrast became a chasm. It was hard now to see how the "practical arts" could serve the "fine arts;" rather, the two were perceived as existing and operating on entirely separate planes. The practical arts were identified as pursuing their own mindless ends, such as bomb-building, manipulating populations through conditioned reflexes, and rendering cities less human or enjoyable to live in. On the other side, the fine arts seemed to exist in large part to denounce what the practical or engineering arts were doing, and to lament their own fate of being linked to, or imprisoned within, this coarse, insensitive, brutal, and irrational psychic sibling—as if, in *The Tempest*, Ariel were somehow bound with Caliban by an invisible cord. Each existed in its own realm, unable to speak a common language to the other, and yet also unable to break away definitively, and was thus condemned to live for all eternity twinned in this strange and uneasy partnership. Thrilling to the dulcet timbre with which Lawrence Olivier gave beautiful baritone expression to Hamlet's *Weltschmerz*, the New Critics wept as they discerned their own fate behind the sorrow of the melancholy Dane:

> O that this too, too solid flesh would melt,
> Thaw, and resolve itself into a dew!
> . . . .
> How weary, stale, flat, and unprofitable
> Seem to me all the uses of this world!
> Fie on't! O fie! 't is an unweeded garden.

That grows to seed; things rank and gross in nature
Possess it merely.

(act 1, sc. 2)

During the Eisenhower fifties, New Criticism was in the service of a conservative ethos, although we have come to see its radical potency in the movements which have come after it, but which were hidden under its mantle, so to speak—expanding its program, or pushing to a limit the aforementioned opposition. At that time, every progressive English teacher brought to class his copy of John Ciardi's *How Does a Poem Mean?* We were all schooled in, drilled on, and became sensitized to the "heresy of paraphrase," from which we learned that the complex resonances, the multiple reflex insights and ironies of poetry simply cannot be captured in the dull, flat, tone-deaf, monotonous idiom of prose. The communications of poetry were otherwise ineffable; they could not be achieved through any other medium. This conviction served to deepen the chasm between the fine and practical arts beyond what Aristotle had imagined or would have understood.

When those of us trained in New Criticism actually got around one day to reading the *Poetics* in its (brief) entirety, the result was somewhat sobering and deflating. Most prominently, we missed the attitude of high seriousness, the conviction of an atoning, or rather a redeeming cultural value to art, which we had grown accustomed to receiving from both the content and the prose style of a long line of late nineteenth and early twentieth-century literary theorists, from Ruskin, Morris, Pater, Matthew Arnold, A. C. Bradley, Gilbert Highet, down to Edith Hamilton.[1] Should religion, and later science, fail us, we nonetheless still believed we had art to save us, to give meaning and value to our lives. No matter how shallow, empty, or corrupt our lives might otherwise become, we could at least come to *know* and express the painful truth about ourselves and our condition—through art. That constituted a permanent possibility of undeniable, inherent value, a final, desperate trump card we could play when we emerged, in the modern project to hyper-suspicion, on the far side of pessimism; something no one could deny or take from us, something that kept our pessimism from becoming truly complete, the concealed promise of a small, but important final victory—and a last chance to save our pride.

Aristotle, by contrast, has a less exalted view of art. He seems to have approached comedy and tragedy much as he approached everything else—as a naturalist. In contrast to the above-mentioned writers, Aristotle feels no particular need to commend or to praise the art he is describing; he is not in the first instance concerned to justify or attack anything. He sees himself rather as confronting a popular phenomenon of disputed purpose and of controversial effect. Something is evidently going on; he simply means to find out what it is. The fact that he studies them does not even imply that these dramas are a good thing. The modern notion of redemption through art represents a need, and comes from a worldview, foreign to Aristotle's; it places a burden and a compensatory task upon art which Aristotle would believe that art is neither required nor able to discharge.

For Aristotle, life has its own rewards, at least when it is well lived. These may well include art, but on the other hand, art notoriously may lead in either of two directions, up or down, as Plato warns, and so one must exercise caution when approaching each new phenomenon. For Aristotle, we cannot be confident about a life beyond this one, but there is excellence to be found even here. It is such excellent activities that provide the joys and pleasures that justify or make life here worthwhile.

Further, the pleasures which accompany successful or complete activities are good for us. It is one of Aristotle's clear claims that tragedy offers its own distinctive kind of pleasure. However, in the *Nicomachean Ethics*, he identifies the pleasure we may feel at the downfall of a good man as vicious (1108b6), so apparently the acceptance of the tragic pleasure should not be as straightforward or unproblematic as it may at first seem; on the contrary, it should be worrisome and is potentially objectionable. Within his own theory, in other words, the burden of proof would seem to fall on tragedy to show why its pleasure is not vicious or injurious to us. In view of this ambiguous and controversial nature of tragedy, one might expect some discussion about the "astounding" impact and almost *sui generis* pleasure (that accompanies the spectacle of the downfall of a great man, and also the impeachment of the good name of the gods)—an attempt to situate and justify this tragic pleasure within Aristotle's vision of the virtuous development of the individual. No such discussion is presented in the *Poetics*.

In his philosophy, art receives a first, modest excuse in view of our creaturely condition under the rubric of a necessary diversion and harmless amusement. It receives a stronger justification from delivering a pleasure—of having, in the case of tragedy, an "astounding" impact on its audience and also delivering an apparently justifiable form of pleasure; and it receives a third justification through Aristotle's claim that art is closer to philosophy than history, that is, that art is the medium by which the universal "comes to stand," or first begins to emerge in the mind out of a host of particulars. In contrast to the late romantic view, art is explicitly not the highest value or activity in civilization for Aristotle—contemplation is. Although questionable or controversial in itself, tragedy might perhaps be defended and justified as an incentive to the highest activity. One might then expect to find in the *Poetics* a discussion specifically of how comedy and tragedy might contribute toward virtuous activity in general, and contemplation in particular. Again, no such discussion is given.

Aristotle's modest concern in the treatise seems to be that, in the interests of building up his science of man, he must spread his empirical net wide enough to catch such phenomena as poetry and drama, as among the significant data to which any theory adequate to this subject must deal. Somewhat analogously to Levi-Strauss and the structuralists of our own day, he seems to assume that poetry and drama are doing *something* interesting or significant for their audience; otherwise these plays would not be as popular as they are. His concern is to determine exactly what job they might be carrying out for people. From an accurate scientific description, almost immediately or without further comment, it should be clear whether this thing is good or bad for them. It is evident that in the *Poetics* Aristotle's attitude toward tragedy and comedy is positive. However, the *Ethics* suggests that the tragic pleasure, although intense and distinctive, is also ambiguous and perhaps dangerous. One does not emerge, in other words, from Aristotle's writings with a clear idea of *why*, or even *if*, the tragic pleasure is good for us.

In contrast to the luxuriant and effusive romantic style, Aristotle approaches poetry in a plain and matter-of-fact way, as simply one more thing in the empirical realm to which he must sooner or later get around. His mode of study is not to isolate and plunge deeply into the internal structural properties of a single dramatic work, but rather to circle cautiously around the phenomena, and in an ordered, newly minted "scientific" approach, to list the subject's genus and species, mention its parts, and hazard a guess as to its possible final cause, or that which it is good for, as its defining traits. His interest may have been drawn to drama initially by the negative evaluation given by Plato, or perhaps was awakened and heightened by the impressive productions in drama during his own life span, the twilight of the all-too-brief "Golden Age" of Pericles in Athens. Socrates is said to have frequented the tragedies of Euripides; Aristotle calls Euripides the "most

tragic" of poets. Aristotle's *Poetics* is seasoned with references to individual plays, some now lost, and he apparently committed many lines and phrases to memory. He
was evidently not insensitive to the charms and attrac-
tions of poetry, although he here tries to put on his "white
coat" and to approach these plays objectively, dispassion-
ately, "scientifically." In contrast to the theoretical and
doctrinaire dismissal delivered by Plato, Aristotle seems
determined to carry out here an open, unbiased, and
empirical examination of the effects comedy and tragedy
actually do have upon their audiences.

And yet, Aristotle does not succeed in giving us the
scientific treatment of drama he promises. Comedy and
tragedy are defined, but the role of each in the life of the
individual, the positive contribution they could make in
the development of the person and to the smooth-running
of the state, though hinted at occasionally, are not ren-
dered nearly as fully as they might be. The impression
given is that, once committed to the project, Aristotle may
have discovered something halfway through his examination that made him start, hesitate, and that finally kept
him from giving the complete or full explanation of his
subject he had at first intended, and perhaps has the
resources to provide. This unsatisfactory situation has led
some commentators to hypothesize that Aristotle may
have panicked and fled before the problem put forward by
tragedy, that he suffered a "failure of nerve" when forced
to confront the underlying source of tragedy's attraction
and power. The hesitancy and avoidance in Aristotle's
treatment of tragedy are undeniable, and a bit surprising;
however, we shall suggest an alternative reason for them.

Aristotle's reluctance to go into these topics may not
have been due to a fear or failure of nerve generated before
the intensity and power of the tragic vision (which he
seems on the contrary to have enjoyed), but perhaps was
due rather to the fact that these topics lay close to, or put
him in mind of, a more objective embarrassment and more

serious failure, which was the inability of his philosophy to complete its own self-given program of generating a complete explanation for the world.

Aristotle projected an ultimate or "master" science of "Being qua Being," a complete explanation of the physical world expanded in the fourfold directions of causality: material, formal, efficient, and final. At the same time that he projects an ultimate efficient cause, he discovers, in the theological sections of the *Metaphysics*, that god can attend to no object or perform no act beyond himself; he is the pure act of thinking fixed upon himself. Any other object of his attention would make him less than he might be and no longer pure act. God thus falls necessarily into a narcissistic self-enthrallment, appropriately fixed upon the highest object around—himself—but becoming thereby a useless "black hole" in the metaphysical heavens and in our attempts to deliver a "first cause" that can function as an ultimate source for the universe. God can function adequately as a *final* cause apparently, but not as a first *efficient* cause for the world. He appropriately absorbs all energy generated within the universe toward himself, but radiates nothing back toward anyone else. In fact, there should *be* nothing else; why there is is a mystery. In sum, Aristotle discovers that he can reason legitimately *up* from the moving world to a nonmoving full substance needed to explain it, but that he cannot reason in the other direction, from the first substance down to a derivative world. Like Parmenides, he is stranded at the top; god could not produce a world. The world thus becomes an ultimate surd, and Aristotle's project to construct a complete explanation for the world must declare bankruptcy or be abandoned.[2]

Faced with this distressing but apparently definitive development, Aristotle does not face up to the difficulty, but rather attempts to camouflage his failure by redirecting and restricting inquiry into efficient causality to the horizontal frontier, limiting it to *this* world, and indeed to each species. Further, and against Plato, he declares the world of motion eternal (*Phy.*, Bk. III, ch. 4–8, Bk. VIII, ch. 1; *Meta.*, Bk. XII, ch. 6). By this maneuver (not unlike Kant's transcendental rebuttal of the cosmological argument for god's existence), Aristotle reverses himself, he absorbs and indeed mobilizes the notion of an "actual infinity" in the natural or phenomenal order to deny the need for a first efficient cause: we can never run through an actual infinity, so we never get to, and need not postulate or produce, a first member of the species to start it off. By tolerating what he had earlier disavowed—an "actual infinity" in the physical order—Aristotle hopes to block the way to (and need for) a first efficient cause. He intends thereby to keep the order of dependency narrowly restricted to the natural or moving realm, closed off from the supersensuous or metaphysical order. By this maneuver, he plans to keep the failure of his system to hold up one corner of the essential fourfold pattern of causality from coming into view. If efficient causality is limited to the phenomenal order, and indeed to each species, and if the world is eternal, then by definition there is and can be no "first efficient cause." The world has always been there, and the species have always been the way they are. The question of "being," provocatively distinguished from the *formal* properties of a creature or derivative substance in the logical and physical works, is dissolved and covered over in the metaphysical works, transformed into the search for an ultimate avatar or primogenitor of the species, which turns out to be nonexistent and unneeded. Once it is seen that the world is eternal, it should also be seen that the request for such a first efficient cause is out of place and inappropriate, and the search for it should properly be given up. The question should dissolve like a will-of-the-wisp, and in this manner Aristotle hopes to disguise the failure of his philosophy to live up to his own program.

The world is left dangling. Either it is, as mentioned, an

ultimate surd, an irrational upsurge without source or sufficient reason, or it is unreal and sheer illusion, in which case, of course, it needs no explanation (as a separate reality). As a last resort, and by default, the world can only be explained as an unintended but necessary side effect of God's self-contemplation, in which case its reality as distinct from God again becomes compromised. The world is absorbed into God's nature, as a necessary part of his self-unfolding. God could not exist without producing a world; the world becomes part of god. This last possibility will be mobilized five hundred years later by Plotinus in his theory of successive "fulgurations" or "emanations" from the "One," which is perhaps the most impressive and best known attempt within the Hellenistic set of assumptions and canons of divine perfection to address this outstanding *lacuna* and never resolved deficiency within the Greek project, and to complete the Aristotelian program of explanation.

Thus, the gods are the ultimate causes of the world, and yet the gods cannot produce a world. The problematic and destabilized relation between the gods and men is also the topic with which tragedy deals. Tragedy pushes us to confront the divine nature and the inscrutable divine will, not necessarily through wonder, but rather (because of our resistance) through terror and dread. What philosophy urges us toward gently with the "carrot" of the pleasure that should accompany the highest knowing, tragedy forces us toward with the unsubtlety of a "stick" by making us confront a horrible alternative. This is one topic in his philosophy that Aristotle does not want to attend to too closely because on his theory, there can be *no* relation between the gods and men—not just on the level of communication or friendship, as he says explicitly in the *Ethics* (1159a5), but also on the deeper level of efficient causality or creation, which he keeps quiet about and attempts to cover over by declaring the world eternal. The world *must* be eternal, or have no need of a cause. He has no other choice.

It must be admitted that tragedy raises this topic in dramatic or personal terms, whereas Aristotle's philosophy considers the issue through abstract and philosophical categories. Nevertheless, tragedy gives rise to reflection, at times to abstract reflection, and it may be that the one question was perceived by Aristotle to be sufficiently near to or translatable into the other, that it would likely put his audience in mind of, or on the trail of, the crucial weakness and most serious vulnerability of his own system. Perhaps because of this, although he feels he cannot overlook tragedy altogether, after a certain point he breaks off his engagement, and his treatment remains formal, external, technical, or "unphilosophical" as Walter Kaufmann describes it.[3] He holds tragedy at arm's length, and, although he is correct in everything he says, he chooses not to go to the deepest issue or to the heart of the matter. He seems to skirt the central provocation, although what he says about the impact of tragedy on the psychological level cannot be gainsaid or contradicted.

Having pointed out this limitation or incompleteness, we hasten to suggest that there may be resources within the Aristotelian corpus for dealing with comedy and tragedy in a more adequate way, for fitting tragedy and comedy into his scheme or design of proper human development, and also to explain how these function as aids for the smooth-running of the state. In particular, there may be resources for accounting for the surprising utility of tragic experience for propelling the individual along a trajectory toward the highest stage of epistemological development. Such a fact would be surprising because in Aristotle's scheme this final wisdom should acquaint us with a deity who is admittedly self-centered, distant, and aloof, but *not* malicious, unpredictable, or irrational—not the "unthinkable" god of tragedy.

We will attempt to show what these resources are, and how comedy and tragedy may contribute, in perhaps strange and unexpected ways, to this virtuous development of the individual.

When one has discerned the deep formal inadequacy within Aristotle's philosophy, and found a way either to correct it or put it to one side so that one is no longer embarrassed or disconcerted by it, one is then in a position to appreciate the resources Aristotle has within his philosophy, had he not turned aside prematurely, for recognizing, exploiting, and utilizing the "blasphemous" theology thrust directly and insistently before our attention by tragedy, resources which explain why tragedy should not be expelled as a pernicious and injurious danger to the body politic (as was urged by Plato), but rather valued and institutionalized as a precious spur and rare incentive to propel individual citizens to higher stages of virtuous development than they would otherwise attain or be inclined to attempt. One comes away not only conscious of Aristotle's deep failure, but impressed also with his astute discovery of the effect of tragedy, and with his open, agile readiness to incorporate the paradoxical utility of the terrifying tragic experience in the service of his nontragic philosophical wisdom.

1

The Contemporary Attack

Theorists have long been intrigued by the brief form and curt style of the *Poetics*. Aristotle's definition of tragedy in chapter 6 as "the imitation of an action that is serious and also, as having magnitude, complete in itself; in language with pleasurable accessories, each kind brought in separately in the parts of the work; in a dramatic, not in a narrative form; with incidents arousing pity and fear, wherewith to accomplish its catharsis of such emotions" (tr. Bywater) has precipitated a veritable library of commentary. Since the time of Nietzsche and later Freud, however, a new edge has appeared in some of this criticism. From this more radical perspective, the objection to Aristotle's treatment of tragedy has moved beyond charges of its being terse, undeveloped, or overly succinct, to the more serious charge that Aristotle, like Plato, was psychologically incapable of handling the irrational world view that tragedy presents, and that as a consequence his theory is seriously flawed at its most fundamental level.

Thinkers have also been puzzled by the mechanical view taken of the tragic effect, as the "arousal of pity and fear, and the catharsis (expulsion) of the same emotions." This terse appreciation is more puzzling in view of the fact that there are arguably resources within Aristotle's anthropology and psychology for a more subtle and sophisticated treatment of how tragedy achieves its distinctive pleasure. Why would Aristotle forego the opportunity to develop a richer and more satisfying discussion of these topics? While it is true that some of his treatises are necessarily curt and succinct because they are most likely notes for lectures, periodically updated, the *Poetics*, in its unhurried and more leisurely style, has the appearance of a freestanding, if unfinished, work, relatively devoid as it is of the systematic references that interrelate the other treatises. Thus there seems less excuse for neglecting this opportunity for a fuller treatment.

Of course, we must be careful to avoid reading modern views concerning the independence and autonomy of art, parallel with a brutally irrational or deterministic view of nature, anachronistically into the Greek setting. The romantic elevation of art to man's highest activity, the isolation of the imagination as the faculty by which man either escapes from or imposes temporary order upon an inchoate nature, identified ultimately as an indifferent or casually violent will, arose during the nineteenth century, where it was influentially thematized in the philosophies of Schopenhauer and Nietzsche. However much such a view may have become the received or mainstream position, the Greek experience was different, and in fact describes a contrary development.

With the defeat of the titans and the ascendancy of the Olympian gods, the Greeks came to have a heightened confidence in a rational foundation for reality, even if this confidence was mythologically expressed. Further, and unlike the modern experience, the rise of "philosophy" served to strengthen rather than to undercut this faith in reason. The development of critical reason during the Greek Enlightenment attempted to purify the myths while retaining the conviction in a rational seat or principle acting behind and through appearances. This stands in contrast to the results of the modern Western Enlightenment, where in a thinker such as David Hume, reason undercuts faith even in itself. Kant and the German idealists reattain a sense of confidence in reason only at the cost of severing all connections between reason and any independent reality. Reason controls only what it itself produces. As a result, the prospect of an independent reality, never fully banished, begins to appear dark and foreboding. This consequence of the Kantian "solution" was developed in the philosophies of Schopenhauer and Nietzsche.

In his defense, it can be argued that there was no reason for Aristotle to regard this irrationalist worldview as a serious alternative to his own thesis that the ultimate substance is rational and benign, if necessarily aloof, distant, and self-enclosed. In our position as heirs to the modern Enlightenment's self-evisceration, Aristotle's faith in reason may appear to some quaint and innocent, a vestige of a beautiful if naive prelapsarian trust from which we have been rudely expelled by the modern Enlightenment's disastrous experiment in hyper-criticism. Given the disappointing and disturbing results of the latter, we understandably look back nostalgically toward the Aristotelian view, while at the same time we are reluctant to give up the perquisites we have acquired by being moderns—the chains we have gotten used to and actually come to enjoy—the exhilarating narcotic of a right to permanent scepticism, and a correlative claim to complete autonomy—traits that bar a serious return to Aristotle's world view or understanding of philosophy. For the time being (as W. H. Auden titles his Christmas oratorio), modern philosophy appears trapped in a state of paralysis, unable to progress either way out of this predicament. Perhaps, as Paul Ricoeur says, we need to move *through* this hyper-critical result to a new, "post-critical naiveté," where contact and trust in an independent reality would no longer be threatening or psychologically intolerable.[1] The alternative, as Gerald Graff (among others) has pointed out, is to persist in a modern Enlightenment victory that turns out to be empty, a triumphant celebration of autonomy achieved at the same moment as total isolation, the spectacle of reason moving toward an exhilarating stage of god-like completion that is simultaneous with complete alienation, leading to political and social irrelevance.[2]

Although its historical influence is granted by all, for some Aristotle's *Poetics* can today only be read from an antiquarian point of view. The irrationalist view has become more and more the mainstream position as the works of Schopenhauer and Nietzsche have influenced Heidegger, Sartre, Derrida, and their imitators and students. The modern Enlightenment has observed a reversal of the triumph of the Olympian gods, and a reinstatement of the titans, or willful, irrational powers, as the ultimate reality. While on the one hand we may not fairly tax Aristotle with not taking seriously a point of view with which he was unacquainted or that he thought had been superseded, still, it can be argued, he should have been more sensitive to the interior dynamic of tragedy, to how it can make use of the irrationalist worldview and indeed forces its audience to confront it, even if tragedy does not insist that we convert or embrace it. Why should he have ignored this source of tragedy's attraction and power? What is it about this dynamic that may have put him off?

An important contribution to the contemporary interpretation of tragedy has been made by the French philosopher, Paul Ricoeur. In his *The Symbolism of Evil*, Ricoeur presents evil, variously conceived as violence or disorder, as a primary topic of the literatures of ancient peoples. Evil received, however, different treatments or explanations at the hands of different cultures. Ricoeur presents in particular the treatment of evil in the theogonic myth of the Sumero–Babylonian culture, and then discusses the way this account was modified in three later explanations of the origin of evil: in the Greek Orphic religion, the Hebrew myth of the Fall, and in Greek tragedy.

According to Ricoeur, the Sumero–Babylonian myth

indicts the gods themselves as the source of evil. Evil is older than creation, older even than the more recent gods, who are born out of a primeval divine conflict. Man is a late arrival and a spectator to this titanic contest. As a matter of fact, man is made from the corpse of a vanquished god, and is indeed brought into being precisely to take the place of the defeated divinity as servant to the victor. This is a theology where violence, passion, and irrationality are defining characteristics of the gods. Man's situation is grim, but at least this theology lets man off the hook in the sense that he is in no way responsible for the introduction of evil into the world—it arrived here ahead of him. Man is relegated to being an observer on the side lines to this chthonic rivalry and battle for supremacy between jealous cosmic powers. If he behaves violently himself, he is merely passing on what he has first received, and he can even invoke the example of the gods as a justification for his own violent conduct.

According to Ricoeur, two of the three later solutions attempted to shift responsibility for evil toward man and to exonerate the gods. In the Greek cosmogonic myth, Zeus and the rest of the Olympian generation learn from the mistakes of their ancestors, and introduce reason and respect into their mutual relationships. The older, violent generation, known as the titans, is not definitively overcome, however; they survive behind the scenes to appear occasionally and cause trouble. Man in particular has a dual ancestry, being made from ashes which are a mixture of an Olympian (Dionysius) and a titan. Thus man has tendencies in two directions, to both good and evil, and can become himself an initiator and independent source of evil.

In the second reaction, the Hebrews, transported to Babylon and forced to confront the polytheistic and violent theology of their captors, carried forth their Exodus faith in the God of Moses and fashioned an alternative creation story out of elements common to the Near Eastern consciousness as an almost point-by-point refutation of the Babylonian creation drama. This has come down to us as the first chapter of the book of Genesis. The world was not made from the corpse of a dead titan, nor indeed was it born of any conflict at all. God is unique and alone at the outset, and if something besides him comes into existence, this can only be because of a free decision, an act of will and intention on his part. Against the Babylonians, God and the world he made are specifically declared good. Man, together with the serpent (a leftover from the Babylonian mythic consciousness, perhaps a local variant of the Greek "titan"), is responsible for introducing evil into the world. The Hebrews have in one sense achieved a more optimistic fundamental theology, one in which God is both rational and benign, but at the cost of making man an independent source and hence a responsible party for the presence of evil in the world.

The third literary genre to take up the problem of evil was Greek tragedy. It is the conviction of Ricoeur and others, however, that there is a variation among the tragic authors in their treatment of evil. Aeschylus, the inventor of tragedy, had fought in the battles of Marathon and Platea, participating in the definitive defeat of the Persian invader. In Aeschylus's trilogies, there is an overall pattern of optimism that both men and gods may grow in control over their irrational passions and wounded self-esteem, and thus also in their flexibility in dealing with other aggrieved parties. In the conclusions of both the *Oresteia* and the *Prometheus* trilogies, for example, there is the clear suggestion that a rational solution can be found to replace conflict, a process of arbitration and compromise that would ultimately make suffering and tragedy itself unnecessary. The only serious moral fault that this tragedy excoriates, according to Walter Kaufmann, quoting from the *Iliad*, is to be "adamantine and unyielding" (T&P, 210).

But as the Athenian peace stretched out, the initial

idealism drifted imperceptibly into a smug complacency. Intrigue and corruption replaced civic pride and a spirit of self-sacrifice, and correlatively this earlier faith in the potential for respect, flexibility, and rationality in both gods and men was gradually eroded. In Sophocles's *Oedipus* and *Antigone*, the gods (and in fact all authority figures) are either absent or display a questionable conduct. By the identity of indiscernibles, in their practical effects, the drama plants the pointed suggestion that whatever gods or fates there are may be conspiring to torment man. A quotation from Shakespeare, who in this respect is close to Sophocles, sums up this outlook forcefully:

> Like flies to wanton boys are we to the gods;
> They kill us for their sport.
>
> (*King Lear*, act 4, sc. 1)

Finally, in Euripides, the doubt initially aroused toward the heavens has ripened into a full cynicism and black, poisonous despair undercutting faith in man's capacity for a noble reaction to the unprovoked and outrageous divine conduct. After that, in the short span that remains of the Periclean "Golden Age," the Greeks could write only comedy, that is, dramas about men "a bit below the average." The depiction of men "above the average" apparently struck them as naive or unrealistic—straining credulity. If for Aeschylus tragedy would ultimately be unnecessary because of the triumph of reason, after Euripides tragedy was similarly impossible, but now due to an opposite development, the loss of faith in reason and of belief in the nobility of either god or man.

Thus, if Greek tragedy constitutes a third solution to the problem of evil, for Ricoeur it is a regressive solution; that is, instead of shifting the responsibility for evil from the gods onto human shoulders, as had the Orphic and Adamic myths, tragedy works in the reverse direction, it constitutes a surprising return to the Sumero–Babylonian theology of identifying and indicting the gods as the ultimate source of evil. This identification is the chief reason for its shock value; that is, against the recently cultivated Olympian piety, the "Apollonian" depictions and rational expectations about the gods, tragedy delivers a counter-portrait that forces us to confront a horrible alternative. This is chiefly responsible for its power to simultaneously fascinate and horrify its audiences. Greek tragedy presents what Ricoeur calls an "unthinkable" or "blasphemous" theology, one not tolerable at the level of explicit creed or a set of propositions, which the mind would find immediately repellent and forcefully reject, but only bearable as an allegory or exotic myth, a story about something happening to someone *else*, where the aesthetic distance thereby generated protects us from its more direct or threatening aspects, but allows us nonetheless to explore its vision, to indulge our curiosity and to contemplate, in relative safety and without negative social pressure or censure, this outrageous or cognitively unacceptable hypothesis.[3] Our minds may have occasionally drifted toward this hypothesis in the past, but if it was entertained at all, it was probably not socially expressed because it constitutes a heresy antagonistic to every piety and to every form of orthodoxy, one that is socially offensive, and upsetting to our most fundamental ways of thinking. Tragedy thus serves the audience as did the shield given in the myth to Perseus—a shield whose polished inner surface would serve as a mirror, reflecting the face of the gorgon, a monster so horrible its view could freeze a man's blood and turn him to stone. If the ultimate reality is irrational, art can go where the mind is defeated or too weak. Art can reflect the terrifying in a psychologically tolerable way. What cannot be viewed *directly* can be glimpsed *indirectly*, and even enjoyed— through art. This, of course, is Schopenhauer's and Nietzsche's philosophy of tragedy, and it is the reason why, for them, art constitutes man's highest and noblest activity—*above* contemplation, science, and certainly religion (which for them is an opposite use of the imagination, to generate consoling fantasies). In this late romantic view, art is the means by which man may turn and achieve the most intimate, direct, and accurate vision of ultimate reality as is possible for us. Art can go where thought cannot venture, where ultimate reality becomes literally unthinkable. One must turn to Schopenhauer and Nietzsche to find commensurate prose descriptions of such a terrifying fundamental principle. Before the nineteenth century and the latter stages of the romantic movement, such descriptions simply had not been produced. Tragedy forces us to confront, to use Herman Melville's words in *Moby Dick*, that divinity whose "right worship is defiance."

The charge against Aristotle by Walter Kaufmann, reflecting Nietzsche, is that, interestingly enough, he ignored or overlooked precisely the "philosophic" dimension of tragedy, that is, the irrational and disconcerting vision that tragedy forces before us and that accounts principally for the power and fascination tragedies have always exercised over people. Instead, Aristotle tries to divert attention to formal or technical matters such as the diction, music, spectacle, etc. Even when he considers plot, which he declares to be the most important element for producing the tragic effect, Aristotle tones down or deliberately misdescribes the most effective plot, so as to avoid carefully the more disheartening and terrifying tragic world view. For example, Aristotle specifies that the hero must not actually be "great" or unqualifiedly good because the spectacle of a good person going from good to bad fortune most people find shocking, discouraging, and repellent. Instead, Aristotle describes the hero as only a "bit above average" (1453a5) (although in the next paragraph he retreats a bit from this restriction and allows that the hero may be greater than that).

Kaufmann contends, to the contrary, that the hero in Greek tragedy is unqualifiedly good. The theory of the tragic "mistake" or "flaw" is an Aristotelian invention without foundation to make the hero's responsibility for his fate more ambiguous, and to spare Aristotle the prospect of a great man being arbitrarily and cruelly struck down by the gods, a plot which contradicts his Apollonian theology—itself, for Kaufmann, an exercise in wishful thinking (T&P, sect. 15). Measured against the *mores* of contemporary Greek society, especially for a person of his high social rank, nothing that Oedipus does would be considered immoral or improper. On the contrary, if he had acted otherwise when he was insulted by Laius's men on the road to Thebes, *that* would have been improper and unacceptable. The great can and should be sensitive to slights to their honor as even Aristotle says (1124b19). As Hamlet later puts it:

> Rightly to be great
> Is not to stir without great argument,
> But greatly to find quarrel in a straw
> When honor's at the stake.
>
> (act 4, sc. 4)

A man of the highest virtue *("megalo-psychia")* enjoys affecting an easy camaraderie and familiarity with servants and underlings designed to put them at their ease (also because their opinions are not worth all that much), but from peers and those closer to him in rank, he demands recognition and respect. For both men and gods, attention and emotion should be proportional to their object. It is a mistake to attend or love an object beyond its worth—but also *below* its worth (1158b25–29). It is wrong to have a low estimate of yourself (unless you really are inferior, and then you should be working to raise yourself), and right to have a high estimate. If your high estimate of yourself is appropriate, or based on an accurate inspection, then you should correctly expect others whose vision is accurate to have a similarly high estimate of you. Both Aristotle and Oedipus live in an unabashedly elitist and hierarchical world. A man should be conscious of his rank and jealous of his reputation, strive to live up to his past repute with his present accomplishments, and finally demand from others the recognition he believes is his due. After all, his reputation is the only thing that will outlive him; it is the only kind of immortality available to him. After being slighted by Laius's men, Oedipus's honor is in jeopardy, and according to the unanimous Hellenic view of the period—including Aristotle himself in the *Ethics*—he has no choice but to fight to avenge the insult to his person and rank. Mock-modesty, playing down, or belittling one's accomplishments is puzzling and vicious behavior for Aristotle, not a virtue, for it bespeaks lack of confidence in either your character or your powers of judgment (1123b11; 1125a20). Either you are not being faithful to your own observations and judgment, or you *are* being faithful, and you really *do not* have the virtue you appear to have. For their own protection, your friends will interpret your puzzling behavior in the latter sense, and avoid relying upon you in a dangerous situation, but either way you are wrong, or not up to what you can and should be. Thus, for Kaufmann, the "tragic flaw" theory is an illusion that Aristotle invented to spare himself what is precisely the most tragic plot line because he found these reflections too troubling, this tragic metaphysic psychologically unbearable.

Aristotle gives himself away further, to Kaufmann, by revealing his preference for melodrama, or plots that seem to involve the spectre of danger, to make our hearts momentarily beat faster, only to be reliably followed by a happy ending. Specifically, Aristotle finally admits in chapter 14 that to his mind the best tragic plot is not even that of an "above average" person experiencing a catastrophe, but rather the plot where one person is on the verge of committing violence against another, but learns the truth of the situation in time to avert the deed (1454a5). Thus calamity or suffering can be avoided altogether, and not only produce tragedy, but apparently produce the *best* of tragedies. This preference is mentioned by Kaufmann as further evidence for Aristotle's failure of nerve and psychic inability to face the plot line of undeserved misfortune happening to good people that tragedy forces insistently upon us (T&P, sect. 16).

In his defense, Aristotle could invoke his hierarchical view of potential audiences. He seems to claim that, to a sufficiently refined or sophisticated audience, simply the suggestion, the possibility, or the expectation of great suffering approaching the hero is sufficient to arouse the characteristically tragic emotions and produce the distinctively tragic experience. As he mentions several times to a sophisticated audience, the mere reading of the play should have the same effect as seeing it performed upon the stage [1453b5, 1462a12 & 17]; but not everyone can read. As Dr. Johnson noted two centuries ago, the prospect of one's death in two weeks does concentrate the mind wonderfully. The prospect, in other words, in this case works nearly as forcefully as the reality upon our psyches, or at least borrows some of its power. Apparently, then, the play does not have to depict a calamity for the tragic effect to be produced. It is enough just to have it come close as a distinct possibility and be present in the *minds* of the audience. After all, art is all pretend or illusion anyway, but the great discovery about art is precisely that what appears upon the stage, or at least what is aroused in the imaginations of the audience, calls up the same sort of emotions as it would in actuality. We prepare the same way for both. It is somewhat like vaccinating yourself against a deadly disease with a weakened form of the same bacillus; it was found that tragedy also could do this, and thus can exploit an apparently analogous psychic mechanism. In this type of plot, we get the "tingle" or foreboding of danger and anticipated suffering, and yet have the relief of having the calamity staved off at the last minute, so that our metaphysical, ethical, and aesthetical sensibilities are not strained, dangerously jarred, or seriously upset. The effect on our nervous systems, however, is almost the same as if it had occurred. We have been through a real experience, but mostly in our imaginations, and thus with fewer long-lasting effects. They both can be food for reflection, however—the one as well as the other. Thus, there can be a "psychic advantage" to tragedy, in the service of wisdom, as there can be a "mechanical advantage" in using the pulley or lever for lifting weights beyond our normal strength. Art has the amazing ability to allow us to benefit from an experience without having to go through it directly.

Again, this line of defense relies upon Aristotle's evident and unembarrassed elitism, his sense that there are different strata to society based not so much on wealth or position but on each person's degree of moral and cognitive development. People at the higher stages apparently do not require the shock of the harshest tragic plot— that of the good person being struck down by calamity— to enjoy the distinctively tragic emotion or whatever benefits it is that tragedy can bring to us. People at lower stages of development (all of us initially?) may need a stronger "jolt" or "dose" of tragic experience to be propelled along similar lines of reflection or psychic development, to be benefited in analogous ways. Perhaps there is room and need for both, for two different tragic plots—one for when we are going "up" in our educational development, and the other for when we have reached our acme. We never outgrow our need for, or the utility of, tragedy, but the strength and nature of the tragic experience alters as our psyches evolve, become more flexible and sensitive, just as our palate seems to shift toward the sour tastes as we mature. This sense of social position and individual development fits in well with Aristotle's remarks on "catharsis" in the *Politics*:

> Emotions that strongly affect some souls are present in all to a varying degree; for example, pity and fear, as well as ecstasy. To this last some people are particularly liable, and we see that under the influence of religious music and songs that drive the soul to frenzy, they calm down as if they had been medically treated and purged. People given to pity and fear, and emotional people generally, and others to the extent to which they have similar emotions must be affected in the same way; for all of them must experience a catharsis and pleasurable relief. (1342a 5–15 [tr. Grube])

At the end of the *Poetics*, in discussing whether epic or tragedy is the superior genre, Aristotle similarly distinguishes a vulgar from a better public. With the explicit appeal to and engagement of the emotions, tragedy appears initially to be the more vulgar of the two. However he concludes that tragedy produces the same effect as epic, only in a more unified and concentrated form. Here, as above in the *Politics*, the justification for tragedy seems almost utilitarian. If you need tragedy to get rid of your pent-up emotions, then use it, but the better sorts of people may not require that radical a purge. Aristotle clearly does not isolate or absolutize tragedy. On the contrary, he has a refreshingly sober and practical view of the utility of tragedy in the development of the individual and the smooth-running of the state. Tragedy is definitely not the highest cultural achievement; contemplation is. A stronger Aristotelian endorsement beyond this frankly hydraulic metaphor of expelling vile humors would apparently require that tragedy be linked somehow, or lead to, contemplation. There is the faintest hint of this in Aristotle's differentiation of audiences based on virtuous, and thus cognitive, development. However, this association or coupling of tragedy with contemplation is not developed to any extent in the treatises that have come down to us.

To Kaufmann, Aristotle's well-known definition of tragedy is a study in avoidance—that is, it is more interesting for what it does *not* say than for what it does. By giving the formal elements of tragedy, and by directing our attention to the characteristic emotions of pity and fear, this description, while minimally correct, gives a distorted and mechanical model of the tragic dynamic and avoids discussing what specifically gives rise to these emotions—which is the "blasphemous" or "unthinkable" theology Ricoeur has described above, the heterodox theology that forces us to confront the possibility that the gods may themselves be evil, vengeful, envious, or spiteful beings, and in turn the source of evil in our world. (As a matter of fact, at *Metaphysics* 983a, Aristotle does consider the possibility that "as the poet says, jealousy is natural to the divine power"; however, he then concludes that "the divine power cannot be jealous," quoting Solon's proverb that "bards tell many a lie.") The acceptance of this blasphemous theology would be the end of respect for religion, for all worship of the gods in the traditional sense, and it is also socially subversive, for the gods are seen as lying behind and supporting the political authorities. Questioning the official cult would quickly translate into an attack upon the public officials as well. (This was one element in the dynamic leading to the trial and death of Socrates.) This theology is thus taboo and publically censored or suppressed in every institutional exercise, *except* tragedy.

Kaufmann explains the attraction and power of tragedy in a fashion similar to Freud's explanation of a psychoanalytic cure, that is, through tragedy the audience is put through something like a collective psychoanalytic course of therapy, we are induced to turn and face a worldview which before we may have suspected was true, but which we repress because it is too horrible to endure.

This painful hypothesis remains, however, in the sub-
conscious, and we are not able fully to banish it from our
minds. In tragedy, this hidden and repressed hypothesis
has the chance to reemerge into consciousness in a nonthreatening and socially approved way. Tragedy thus allows us to entertain and confront what we otherwise find
too painful to contemplate directly. This dynamic of the
blasphemous theology would explain on the one hand the
fascination of tragedy as we enter into the play, the reason
our eyes remain fixed upon the hero to see how he reacts
to things, as he begins to undergo his painful "conversion," that is, his gradual, reluctant substitution of a
darker and less attractive hypothesis for his initial optimistic interpretation of his situation—for we see ourselves in him—we see the hero as a stand-in for ourselves.
He is making the same kind of transition we are; we want
to compare his reactions to our own. A great person's
going through it prepares the way and makes it that much
easier for us to do the same. This account would also
explain the "catharsis," the sense of relief and purgation
that Aristotle notices, in a more satisfactory way than his
own hydraulic model of tragedy simply eliminating or
evacuating the emotions of pity and fear that it first
arouses.

Thus far, Kaufmann's interpretation seems both helpful
and correct. What Kaufmann does not mention is that
tragedy can have this beneficial effect, or perform this
service, regardless of whether the tragic vision is the truth
of our situation or not. Specifically, tragedy may still
function as an aid to the viewer in confronting his deepest
fears and suspicions, allowing him to indulge them sufficiently to satisfy his own curiosity and to reach his own
independent conclusion, without the tragic hypothesis
for that reason being true, or the viewer coming to the
conclusion that it is true. Kaufmann moves from the utility of the tragic experience and the *ad hominem* charge of
psychological weakness in those who reject the tragic

vision, directly to the truth of the tragic worldview, a conclusion which does not necessarily follow. One can assent to every observation Kaufmann makes concerning the power and dynamic of tragedy, and even see in his theory a powerful explanation for the utility of tragedy in the psychological development of the individual, without thereby assenting to the tragic view as inevitably the truth of our condition. In fact, one may come to exactly the opposite conclusion. All one can reasonably conclude from his account is that, after the experience of tragedy, we are for the first time in a position to arrive at a rational, noncompulsive, nonmanipulative *decision* about the tragic worldview—to embrace it or to reject it—with a sense of peace and equanimity which before were unavailable or unjustified. Tragedy puts us through an experience in which we can for the first time examine the alternative to our "perennial" optimistic outlook in a nonthreatening way, turn to face our deepest fears, examine them quietly and calmly, and come to our own independent, settled conclusions. Tragedy may be a useful, and for some people even an essential, means to face this irrationalist alternative to the conventional social outlook. What Kaufmann says about the psychological utility of tragedy may be true, but that must not be allowed to prejudice the outcome the individual comes to as he or she moves *through* the tragic experience and emerges on the far side. Kaufmann's contribution is to suggest that tragedy must be appreciated as much as method or process, and not only as a position. He overshoots the mark in concluding from the utility and beneficial effect of being made to face the tragic worldview to its necessary truth. In so doing he extracts a conclusion that is in excess of his data. This alacrity suggests that Kaufmann's own insistent and caustically aggressive advocacy of the tragic vision may spring from unreflected, unconscious, or compulsive psychological forces within which Kaufmann himself is imprisoned—similar to the psychological "backlash" he accuses the nontragic philosophical position of being. Tragedy's utility is psychological, while its purported truth is logical; these are separate and distinct planes of reality. The most the data entitle us to assert is that a person is in a better position to make a free, non-fearful, and nonmanipulative decision about the tragic dimension of reality *after* he or she has been through the aesthetic experience of tragedy than that person was before. Anything further is tendentious, intrusive, and overbearing.

According to Kaufmann, neither Plato nor Aristotle was able to face this irrational alternative that the tragic poets had opened up. Confronted with this view, they experienced a buckling in the knees and a failure of nerve. In fact, what we call "philosophy" began merely as a psychological backlash, a nostalgic retreat or panic-stricken flight into a rationalized version of the old Apollonian theogony, seeking to reinstate by theoretical speculation what tragedy had attacked and routed at the level of conventional myth.[4] For both Nietzsche and Kaufmann, "philosophy" is not an unambiguous development or positive achievement. It is not a manifestation of strength, the unveiling of a new, rational power, but rather testifies to a weakness and *loss* of power among those who could not endure the grim and challenging vision Greek tragedy was rather urgently turning them toward. In this regard, Aristotle is perhaps a bit less reprehensible than Plato in that, in the *Poetics*, he at least shows a greater sensitivity and more correct register of the effect tragedy has upon its audience, and he had the courage to oppose Plato by his contrary claim that tragedy can perform a positive function for the body politic. But however enchanted and attracted to tragedy Aristotle may have been at the aesthetic level, at the conceptual level he again reverted to a safely nontragic position. His metaphysical "unmoved mover" is perhaps not all that our highest or most complete fantasy would have him be; he is distant, aloof, only a final cause for the movement in the cosmos, locked in a narcissistic self-regard and self-enthrallment. He does not care about or even know us, cannot desire to communicate or move toward us. But for all that, he is still not malicious, spiteful, or irrational. God's very aloofness protects us from any direct interaction with him—and this is not so bad; he cannot benefit us, but also he cannot hurt us. This is a question of whether you call the glass half empty or half full. The situation is perhaps not as good as we might like, but still it is considerably better than tragedy shows it might have been.

Thus, for Nietzsche and Kaufmann, Greek tragedy may have given rise to philosophy, but not as a consistent and legitimate extension of its own daring scepticism—rather, by way of reaction and backlash, a psychological rejection of the precise worldview tragedy was opening up. Ironically, tragedy may be considered an offspring and more aggressive or daring extension of the central project of the Greek Enlightenment, the program to purify the myths of anthropomorphisms and fanciful elements, with its sceptical, probing, and fearless temper. Even more ironically, "philosophy" cannot be so considered. In Kaufmann's view, philosophy is an attempt to brake, arrest, and even reverse this progressive, liberating, critical movement. For both Nietzsche and Kaufmann, philosophy was not born through calm reflection upon the irrational alternative which the tragic art made both available and psychologically endurable, but rather constitutes an uncontrolled, headlong flight back toward a rationalized Olympian fantasy, which it erects and invokes as a magical incantation or protective talisman against the tragic worldview which Socrates, Plato, and Aristotle did not have the courage to entertain or contemplate steadily once it had been unveiled and disseminated aesthetically by tragedy.

2

An Aristotelian Response

We have seen Kaufmann's charge against Aristotle's interpretation of tragedy. How might Aristotle respond to this
challenge? If we claim that Aristotle has deeper resources
for dealing with the phenomenon of tragedy than he
chooses to discuss or bring forward, what are they? Specifically, how might tragedy fit into his broader scenario
of psychic and cognitive development in the individual?
For Aristotle, man has a single mind, but it may swivel
between two orientations: it may turn toward the unchanging realm, in its highest theoretical use, or it may
direct itself toward the fleeting and changeable objects
which surround us here below. Theoretical cognition may
be man's highest activity, but he has to first get his practical house in order to obtain the leisure to indulge his
theoretical curiosity. That is, he has to first achieve sta-
bility and security with the changeable objects on which
all life—including the higher life—depends. Aristotle
brings these points together early in the *Metaphysics*:

> For it is owing to their wonder that men both now begin
> and at first began to philosophize; they wondered originally
> at the obvious difficulties about the greater matters, e.g. about
> the phenomena of the moon and those of the sun and of the
> stars, and about the genesis of the universe. And a man who
> is puzzled and wonders thinks himself ignorant (whence
> even the lover of myth is in a sense a lover of Wisdom, for the
> myth is composed of wonders): therefore since they phi-
> losophized in order to escape from ignorance, evidently they

were pursuing science in order to know, and not for any utilitarian end. And that is confirmed by the facts; for it was when almost all the necessities of life and the things that make for comfort and recreation had been secured, that such knowledge began to be sought. Evidently then we do not seek it for the sake of any other advantage; but as the man is free, we say, who exists for his own sake and not for another's, so we pursue this as the only free science, and for it alone exists for its own sake. (982b 12–18)

Man is first of all an animal, even if he is a rational animal. As directed toward changeable objects, his mind builds up practical virtue; as directed toward the unchanging objects, it cultivates intellectual virtue. The practical virtues are complex, involving the interaction of the intellect and the passions, and aim at a mastery by the intellect over the passions, a mastery built up slowly by habit. Theoretical virtue is comparatively simple, involving only the acuteness and accuracy of our cognitive faculty alone, which, however, is also improved by use. The theoretical objects are more intelligible in themselves, but also more removed from our conventional ways of seeing and thinking. Their superior clarity causes them at first to dazzle, blind, and confuse us, so that the effect is the same as if we were dealing with objects which are inherently obscure. As Aristotle says, in doing philosophy we are like owls at midday, dazzled by the sun.

The two virtues, intellectual and moral, are for Aristotle not opposed, but rather complement and even require one another. As mentioned, we must master our life practically to find the leisure to indulge our theoretical interest. Thus, although theoretical activity may be the higher of the two, it is dependent upon and to some extent subordinated to the same mind operating in its practical mode. After all, we cannot think all the time. Contemplation takes its orders and gets its allotted time period from practical reason. In its turn, practical activity is dependent upon the mental clarity and acuity that is cultivated in the mind's purely theoretical use. Practical virtue consists in the ability to see and hit the medium, or appropriate middle, between the extremes of excess and deficiency; it thus presupposes both cognitional development and passional discipline. Practical virtue requires our seeing a "mean" between extremes, a vision which only our intellectual faculty can provide. The repeated attempts to "hit" this mean, and to control our passions, increase both the acuity of our vision as to where this mean lies, and also our ability to hit it easily. The two virtues are thus not rival lines of development, but on the contrary mutually presuppose, involve, and reinforce one another.

The theory of pleasure is perhaps the principal link between Aristotle's ethical and aesthetic theories. Its correct understanding is crucial for explicating the way in which comedy and tragedy might be integrated within Aristotle's overall theory of virtuous development.

For Aristotle the goal of life is happiness; men differ as to the means, but they agree that the end is happiness. Socrates may have believed (and Plato spent the whole of the *Republic* trying to prove) that virtue is not just a necessary, but also a sufficient condition for happiness. According to Aristotle, this position is not realistic. Virtue is certainly a necessary condition for—and the best means toward—happiness, but it is not sufficient. For happiness in the conventional sense, one needs the blessings of good health, attractive features, a successful marriage, comely children, elegant possessions, and finally, virtuous friends with whom to share one's accumulated riches—accessories and embellishments which fortune sometimes allies with virtue, but not always, as Kant pointed out in discussing what he called the *summum bonum*. Saying the same thing on the practical level, to be *humanly* happy, one needs not only virtue, but also pleasure (1153b20; 1177a22). Fortunately, says Aristotle, we are so set up that pleasure normally accompanies virtue. Virtue he defines as the excellent and unimpeded functioning of a capacity. According to Aristotle we are so made that when we attain excellence or virtue in any of our distinctive activities, a pleasure typically "kicks in" or begins to accompany that activity (1153b12). This pleasure both reinforces us in the exercise of that activity, and also spurs us to attain still greater excellence, as a way to experience yet greater pleasure. This is another way in which the Aristotelian universe is benign or nontragic— or good in a way it did not have to be. The Aristotelian god in whose dispensation we happen to be living, who set up the current universe, has made pleasure to accompany, crown, and reward virtue. Of course, there are certain pleasures which are not good for us; not all pleasure is a sign of virtue. This is because certain activities can be done to excess, or in improper circumstances (1173b30). But Aristotle still holds there is a distinctive pleasure that accompanies the proper functioning of each of our activities. We should be grateful; the world could have been set up far differently.

It is interesting to compare Aristotle and Kant on the topic of pleasure. For Aristotle, the ability to take pleasure spontaneously in doing what reason prescribes is the distinguishing characteristic of the virtuous person. Of course, this does not come automatically or effortlessly; it is built up slowly by habit. But unless a person derives pleasure from what he is doing, he is not truly virtuous, but at best "strong-willed"—a term which implies that the passions have not been sufficiently schooled to accept the direction of reason, so that, if the person ends up doing what is right, he does so "gritting his teeth," so to speak, or acting against his "druthers." Pleasure for Aristotle thus accompanies and is the index of virtuous formation (1099a10).

Kant, by contrast, tolerates pleasure, but he is more suspicious of it. An act is virtuous or has moral value for

Kant only if it is done out of respect for the moral law. One's intention must be to follow duty for duty's sake. But how can I be sure I am acting principally out of respect for the moral law—especially if I am *enjoying* what I am doing? While pleasure is a morally neutral sensation, the psychological danger is that pleasure is so attractive to the mind that it often functions as a rival to duty, and thus can easily displace the moral law and usurp the role which duty alone should occupy. Perhaps I am doing what looks like a generous or self-sacrificing act out of a concealed motive of self-love or long-range enlightened self-interest. In practice, then, only if doing an action causes me some pain can I be *sure* that I am not doing it for the pleasure I might be surreptitiously deriving from it, rather than out of respect for the moral law. Kant's position thus comes close to being the opposite of Aristotle's: whereas for Aristotle *only* if I am experiencing pleasure can I be virtuous, Kant would say that only if I am *not* experiencing pleasure can I be *sure* that I am virtuous. If you are enjoying what you are doing, for Kant, what you are doing is probably wrong, or at least has no moral value. Though nominally a Christian, Kant evidently lived under a distinctly harsher dispensation than did Aristotle.

One surprising consequence of Aristotle's theory is that eventually you are responsible for the pleasures you feel (1114b2). You cannot claim that they are spontaneous, or that you are simply made that way. In fact, virtue is defined or empirically specified by Aristotle as schooling yourself to feel the *right* emotion to the right degree at the right time. What to many of us is formed by nature is for Aristotle determined almost exclusively by "nurture," that is, it is a deliberate product of our practical habits (1103a24; 1106a10). As a matter of fact, Aristotle's moral discussion is not concerned primarily with actions at all (he assumes we are all aiming at excellence), but is more subtle or psychological, dealing principally with the pleasures and pains one feels in certain circumstances

(1152b5). Correct action will follow from proper psychological formation, and the proper psychology is itself built up by habits of doing certain kinds of actions in certain situations. Pleasures and pains are spontaneous and morally indifferent only in children. Once we begin schooling ourselves, they become morally significant, indeed decisive and determinative of our moral condition. Actions by themselves are nonspecific, or can signify different characters in different situations. The same is true for some psychological states. For example, a sense of shame Aristotle says is becoming and to be praised in a young person for it shows he is conscious of a level of excellence he is not yet attaining, and is still open to correction and development; in an older, supposedly mature person, however, shame is inappropriate and out of place. By then a person should not be doing anything seriously wrong or worthy of embarrassment. He should be "shameless" in the good sense of not doing anything socially offensive or worthy of censure. A sense of shame in such a person is perhaps better than not caring what one does, but still indicates the absence of a moral development that should have taken place (1128b 15–35).

For Aristotle, you tell whether a person is virtuous or not, not so much by what he does, but by what he *enjoys* doing. Pleasure is thus important to the cultivation of virtue not only as its goal, as a necessary part of happiness, but also in its identification, to test whether reasonable behavior has become hardened by habit so as to be done easily and with enjoyment.

One final point is Aristotle's claim that the pleasure that accompanies a given activity (even the highest activity, such as thinking) is specific to that activity (1175a 23–30). It is unlike the pleasure that accompanies other activities. They are incommensurable, and to this extent Aristotle would be against the "felicific calculus" of the latter-day utilitarians. However, he is experimental, and not doctrinaire on the subject. When they occur together, two pleasures may mix and reinforce one another, or they may impede and interfere with each other. The pleasures of the mind are "purer," he says, but they are typically weaker than those of the body (1176a2; 1177a25). This is crucial for his analysis of drama. For people quite properly come to the theater to be entertained, that is, to receive pleasure. They do not come to be harangued, instructed, or lectured to, even if such might be good for them. If the acting is bad, Aristotle notes, the audience tends to eat more sweets—as if to compensate for what they are not getting, but expected to get, from the stage, and to show their resolve to get their pleasure one way or the other (1175b13). This in fact forms the unspoken compact or agreement between the playwright and his audience. This is why pleasure is a link between Aristotle's ethical and aesthetic theories. The playwright may do whatever he wants, as long as he gives the audience pleasure; the audience, in turn, will take almost anything from the playwright, as long as it gets its pleasure. This opens up extraordinary opportunities for the playwright to construct complicated and sophisticated aesthetic experiences; however, it also puts great demands upon him. In particular, he cannot let his ingenuity or good intentions distract him from his primary obligation. While the "sky's the limit," in a sense, he must still deliver the goods, and the goods are pleasure. Any kind of pleasure will do, but pleasure it must be. There is no adequate substitute or acceptable alternative. The playwright is never allowed to violate this contract, and there are severe penalties to pay if he fails.

According to Aristotle, every complete activity delivers its own kind of pleasure. The unspoken contract with the audience does not commit the playwright to delivering the lowest kinds, or only one kind of pleasure; in fact, it almost seems to require the opposite. For according to Aristotle, the lower pleasures cannot be sustained for very long, and the playwright is committed to supplying a full evening of diversion and entertainment. If he is clever or aspires to have a long career, the playwright must explore the less obvious and more subtle or complicated pleasures available. From the other side, the audience knows that it is not all that easy to deliver an evening full of pleasure, and is thus ready to swallow a lot of other "stuff," or jump through a lot of strange hoops, if thereby it can successfully obtain an appropriate or commensurate amount of pleasure. This is one point of leverage the playwright exercises over his audience: it is his unique entree or point of access into the deepest chambers of their psyches, the lure with which he can get them to move in any direction or go to any place he wants them to. A good playwright is more valuable than gold; the major courts of Europe each had two or three subsidized playwrights. In a sense, each party needs the other, but the audience needs the playwright more. The playwright, after all, can earn his living some other way, but the people can only get their pleasure, entertainment, and enjoyment from people like himself. Expressed simply, he has what they want, and he is the only place they can get it. Pleasure that is copious, intense, and still respectable (so that we are not embarrassed to look at ourselves in the mirror the next morning), is not all that common or easy to come by; on the contrary, it is as rare as diamonds. The public will pay top dollar for it—for themselves, and as a prestigious gift to offer to important guests. In the theater rich and powerful people put themselves in an unusually receptive and vulnerable position before the playwright. At his guidance, moments of the most delicate or subtle psychological examination and extraordinary dramatic power may be orchestrated. The audience is even willing to go through considerable *pain*, if this produces a commensurate payoff in pleasure. It is willing to trust the playwright here. There must be perks along the way to

keep the audience going, however, and of course a final
pleasure kicking in at the end, one that reaches back and
suffuses the whole experience, making the evening satisfying and worthwhile.

The audience hands itself over trustingly to the playwright to be manipulated and even roughly handled, as
we might on occasion deliver ourselves to a bone-crush-
ing masseur, believing that the experience, although perhaps jarring as we go through it, will ultimately be beneficial to us and will even make us feel good. The clever
playwright must mobilize pleasure and pain, as both lure
and whip, to induce the audience to go where it does not
habitually go, where it perhaps normally has every reason
and every intention of not going, to face what it would
otherwise choose not to face. Because of our desperation
for diversion and entertainment, we give the playwright
wide-ranging power, almost unparalleled elsewhere in
society; we accept the manipulation and the difficulty
because we trust the playwright will eventually lead us to
an interesting and perhaps novel pleasure that will more
than compensate for the difficulty, that may even turn the
experience into an awe-inspiring and unforgettable evening. For we know from experience that that is the amazing thing about art: there are no upper limits. The
possibilities of achievement are not preset, but are limited
only by the playwright's ambition, talent, and daring. We
say, in effect, "Amaze us!" and we hope that he succeeds.
Thanks to the skill and daring of the playwright, the pay-
back can sometimes be many times what we were asked to
invest. In this sense, art seems to defy gravity, or to violate
the law of the conservation of energy: the output can
apparently exceed the input. Art is extraordinary, a continuous, inexhaustible nurturer and restorer. It is a minor
miracle, a font of energy, an exception to everything else
in the universe, something that should not be possible,
that is semi-divine. As Robert Browning writes in his
poem *Abt Vogler*:

I know not if, save in this, such gift be allowed to man
That out of three sounds he frame, not a fourth sound, but a
   star.

The very first step—the buying of the ticket—constitutes an act of trust on our part, a step into the unknown. We accept on trust that the greater pleasure may lie ahead, on the far side and through the veil of the unknown, and possibly even through certain painful experiences. We want decent recreation. We feel we have a right to that; we have worked hard for it. Through this embarrassing metaphysical weakness, this craving for diversion, the audience renders itself unusually defenseless, open, and malleable—to the disappointment of failure and catastrophe if the artist fails, but also, it hopes, to benefit from exceptional, dazzling, and powerful moments if he succeeds.

The playwright can do anything he wants to us, take us anywhere he wishes, as long as he gives us pleasure. We are so desperate for diversion, we will agree to face things we normally turn away from—at the very least, they will be *different*, and thus can provide distraction from the routine of our daily lives. And here lies the playwright's opportunity. It is through this, our metaphysical weakness, that both comedy and tragedy gain purchase, breach the wall of our defenses, obtain their first position and power to cause unexpected and powerful explosions in our experience. As viewed from the difficult obligation of the playwright, tragedy and comedy can be appreciated as ingenious and sophisticated solutions to the problem of supplying an evening full of entertainment that is intense and still respectable. They are complex experiments following the lines of this unspoken contract to deliver an intense, rich, and satisfying pleasure through the medium of story. Perhaps to achieve this, the playwright *has* to veer close to what is both real and frightening to us. These topics, after all, have the advantage of being new and also powerfully charged. Further, being distracted by reality, as opposed to being diverted by illusion, lends a dry astringency to the overall experience which precludes or reduces any cloying aftertaste—any sensation of surfeit or oversweetness. If the playwright can find a way to divert us somehow with reality, we get the power of novelty without the element of escape or illusion, and hence without the letdown, the experience of "cold turkey" afterwards, when we have to readjust our perceptions and expectations back to the routine of everyday. Where it can be achieved, understatement is more powerful and effective than overstatement. We are entertained with far less than we normally take to be satisfied. Thus we get the best of both worlds. By inducing us to face what we habitually avoid, we have the experience of diversion and distraction, but we have never left reality. On the contrary, we have been taken "deeper" into it. It is, after all, not the particular note struck, but the contrast and pattern between notes that determines the aesthetic effect.

It may even be true that the comic and tragic solutions, although in one sense remarkable and the indisputable work of genius, are in another sense inevitable and predetermined, the way a mathematical solution is determined by the conditions of the problem it unties, although it might take the human race hundreds of years to find the answer. In other words, perhaps the gradual development of these genres, as Aristotle outlines their evolution, was not an accident, but followed a predetermined and inevitable course, drawn toward certain definite end-positions, and controlled by the parameters of the task of providing intense and respectable forms of pleasure through the medium of story. Although tragedy may incidentally be good for us, its development was perhaps propelled, and its final stage made inevitable, not so much by moral, but rather by purely *aesthetic* forces and criteria. For in the last analysis, it is not so easy to be entertained for an entire evening.

If so, this would not cheapen or lessen the achievement. On the contrary, it would strengthen the claim of these dramas to being unique and precious cultural treasures, to be passed on carefully to our descendants.

Aristotle has said that pleasure tends to accompany any activity done with excellence—even the act of knowing. Also, there is the pleasure, or the release from anxiety, when we finally turn to face some unattractive or painful aspect of our situation, especially one we have been putting off. The clever playwright, whose burden it is to provide an evening's entertainment, must engage this tendency and tap this available, irritable energy by conjuring up a story which daringly mentions or invades precisely these topics, which may then end by awakening long pent-up discontents and frustrations. We are diverted, if by nothing else, by variety, by the release of energy, and by our change of mood. The gamble that the tragic and comic playwright takes is that his skill may not be up to providing forms of pleasure that will more than compensate us for certain admittedly disagreeable forms of awareness he may find necessary to bring us to construct his drama. That is the risk he takes, but like the acrobat (who is also an entertainer), he is in a high-risk profession. The motivation of the playwright may be part desperation, part idealism, part audacity—it makes little difference. Whatever his motivation, this is the direction in which the successful prosecution of his difficult, self-imposed project must inevitably lead him.

3

Comedy and Moral Virtue

Aristotle locates the principles of successful comedy and tragedy at a deeper level of the human psyche than simply the desire for entertainment. All art, he tells us, begins in imitation. As children we take a spontaneous delight in imitation, and this stays with us all our life as the basis upon which all later satisfactions in art build. Imitation well done inspires our admiration because it is difficult, and thus rare. Imitation also seems to be our first form of learning, and according to Aristotle, all people naturally desire to know. There is a particular pleasure—the "Eureka!" experience of Archimedes—that seems to accompany all learning successfully carried out. Thus it should be a self-sustaining process, or something to which we naturally tend. Someone who can imitate something successfully, or well enough to make us think of it, appears to have isolated and understood its basic traits. Imitation thus arouses our admiration as a form of discovery, penetration, and cognitive mastery, besides testifying to muscular agility and control.

Our curiosity is further heightened if the object of imitation is a human being. Besides our admiration for the artist's craft, a more personal interest intervenes here. We do not exist as isolated individuals; rather, we exist among other people, and our lives trace a career or a trajectory which we can compare with those of other people. In particular, our lives can go well or badly, and we do all that we can to make sure they go well. As

Aristotle says, we are all aiming at happiness; for that reason we are all anxious about whether we shall attain it. Consequently, any story which depicts people's lives, especially if it shows them ending well or badly, has a heightened relevance and a more particular interest for us above other forms of imitation. This interest is not born out of idealism or the desire for contemplation. Rather, it is for the most practical or selfish of all reasons: we might possibly learn something we can use. Some of the character, situations, or lessons from these stories might have application to our own lives.

We are anxious in particular in that people can end badly because of things outside their control. Some people catch leukemia and die; others are killed in plane crashes. We want to avoid these things if at all possible, although on a certain level we realize they are beyond our control. However, we seem to enjoy stories which suggest a correlation between a person's behavior and the fate he or she eventually experiences. Perhaps the ground for this is the desire to avenge ourselves against chance viewed as unfair or capricious, or at least some form of self-justification. Besides providing the reassurance of an overall providence in the cosmos, this correlation also implies a type of control we might exercise over our fate. For we *can* choose our behavior, and we may like to think this allows us to guide, albeit indirectly, our ultimate destiny. Whatever its truth, this theory is attractive to us because we think the universe would be better if things ran that way. Good people should do well in this life, and evil people less well. Beyond that, most of us seem to go further and to make an unspoken compact with fate. We will try to be as "good" as we reasonably can be, that is, we agree not to join the "evil" people in the world or to hurt other people excessively. On the other side we expect the gods, or fate, or whoever runs the world, to do all they can to make sure that we are not involved in a fatal plane crash or catch leukemia, or experience any of the other calamities that we know happen to people and that are beyond their control. We recognize upon reflection that this agreement, and the belief on which it is based, are not fully rational, that is, bad things *do* happen to good people. We recognize that the passengers who go down in a plane crash are probably just a random slice of humanity, on the whole no better or worse than you and I. Still, we like to think that there is some correlation between one's goodness and one's ultimate destiny. Further, such a belief and unspoken agreement seem to play a role in our experience of both tragedy and comedy; specifically, in both this agreement arouses our interest and keeps us attached to the story through the suffering we must endure to attain the final satisfaction.

Early in the *Poetics,* Aristotle tells us that there are only four basic plots, with a few variations, out of which all stories are composed. A story must be about a person who is either good or bad, and the person must eventually do well or badly. These are the only four plots there are; these are the only four plots that are *possible.* Every story must be a variation or a combination of these. Aristotle proceeds to explore the inherent dramatic effects which each plot has upon its audience. The story of a bad person finishing well, he says, most people find off-putting because it offends our moral sense. Similarly, he says most people find shocking and objectionable the plot of a good person going from good to bad fortune. The plot of a bad person going from good to bad fortune is more satisfying, and is the substance of many "morality tales" and much didactic literature. This and the "double plot" he mentions in regard to comedy (the good and the bad getting their just deserts, as in Dickens's novels) seem to illustrate the implicit agreement with fortune mentioned above, and to pander to our craving for a moral foundation for the universe, our desire for control over our own destiny, and finally our desire to locate ourselves among the "good" people in history (1453a29). This genre gives a reliable and socially approved pleasure (in fact, he says, less cultivated people even prefer it to the drier pleasure of tragedy), which accounts for its regular following and perennial popularity. The plots of tragedy and comedy Aristotle finds to be complications of two of these types. The protagonist of a tragedy, he says, should be above average, but not "great" or unqualifiedly good, and typically goes from good to bad fortune (although, as mentioned, for a sophisticated audience, he allows the catastrophe to be called off at the final moment, and grants that the tragic effect may still be produced). In comedy, the protagonist should be a bit below the average. In comedy, the suffering is not serious, and the perception of the protagonist as lower than ourselves interjects into our laughter an element of superiority or snobbery that functions as a further cushion or insulating buffer to keep us from excessive suffering. The question we intend to pursue in this chapter is, to what extent is comedy oriented for Aristotle toward practical knowledge or moral virtue, that is, toward things which can be changed (our own conduct) in contrast to tragedy, which (if we follow the parallel) should propel us to contemplate things which cannot be changed, and about which it makes no sense to deliberate—things which are thus relegated to being objects of exclusively theoretical or contemplative interest. We will pursue the question of whether and how comedy may contribute to practical virtue in this chapter, and leave the question of how tragedy may contribute to intellectual virtue, or contemplative knowledge, to the final two chapters.

The comic hero engages in a mild rebellion against social mores; thereby he comes close to serious misfortune, but characteristically recognizes the error of his ways in time to be reconciled to society after only mild suffering. Since both comedy and tragedy involve suffering, and since the audience is encouraged to identify with the protagonist, the problem the playwright faces in both cases is the same. To ride out this suffering, the audience needs some inducement to stay with the story during the difficult moments, rather than to drop off the story or simply walk out. After all, we are not paid to be there; on the contrary, we are paying *him*. Also, we are not masochists; we do not enjoy being made to suffer. The solution is that the playwright must discover an attraction sufficiently powerful to induce the audience to invest emotionally in the protagonist, perhaps even to identify with him. If such a bond can be forged, we will then care what happens to him—because we care what happens to ourselves, and he is now our stand-in. We will want him to succeed, and this desire will help us to stay with the drama to see how it comes out. As with Aristotle's theory of friendship, we will love him as we love ourselves, and for the same reason: we come to see him as another version of ourselves (1166a31).

If this interest can be sparked and this identification forged, then the playwright has us. We will stay with the story. Subsequently, in fact, he must use aesthetic distance to protect the audience against excessive suffering that might incline them to drop away from the story. The playwright thus walks a tightrope, or better, mobilizes and combines carefully two opposing forces: first, emotional investment, to arouse interest in the first place and to induce us to stay with the story; second, aesthetic distance, to insulate us against excessive suffering until the projected pleasure that should accompany a complete activity, and the new knowledge generated by the drama, kicks in and converts what up until then was pain into but a superficial first impression of a considerably more complicated, richer, and denser experience, contributing an arresting and astringent tang to one of the more interesting and satisfying aesthetic experiences.

In comedy, this vicarious identification is supposedly secured by making the protagonist a bit below the average. Why would this be of interest or attraction to us? Why would we be tempted to identify with such a character? Further, is there any tie-in between comedy and our psychic development? How could the depiction of such a low individual assist in the virtuous formation of an individual?

Moral virtue for Aristotle consists in discerning the mean between extremes, and disciplining the passions so as to "hit" the mean regularly and with ease. Society eventually develops norms or rules based on these habits to help develop the individual, to facilitate social exchange, and to protect itself against chaos. We are all socialized into these *mores* as young people. No matter how rational and correct these norms may be, however, according to Aristotle, man's creaturely or derivative status entails that he cannot carry out *any* activity, even the highest and most rational, indefinitely. As material and potential beings, we require alteration or variety to relieve the tedium and monotony of any routine (1176b35; 1127b34). We grow tired, bored, and eventually resentful of an unvarying diet of the same. Comedy seems to come tailor-made for this creaturely condition, a remedy peculiarly suited to our not-fully-substantial status, virtually a gift from the gods to minister to our metaphysical weakness. Specifically, for Aristotle comedy is justified beyond being a harmless diversion by its surprising capacity to play upon this desire for variety and, by a clever manipulation, to convert us to an affective reacceptance of what we previously found boring and intolerable—practical virtue.

Comedy is predicated upon a perceived discrepancy or gap between the demands that society makes, through its rules and norms, and the individual's preferences, his spontaneous feelings, or "druthers." According to Aristotle, the "weak-willed" person is a bit below the average (1152a24), and we note here a similarity with his description of the comic hero, and another potential link, besides his doctrine of pleasure, between his aesthetic and moral theories. In comedy the hero typically engages in a minor rebellion against a social norm felt to be oppressive. We in the audience have on occasion chafed under such a rule, have found it confining or constraining, although out of concern for our reputation and social position, we perhaps do not admit publically to such feelings. But with the comic protagonist, it is a different story. He is a scamp, a scallywag, a rascal and scapegrace—a low-class fellow who has no particular position to save or reputation to protect, and who can thus act on such feelings with less inhibition and more abandon. On the other hand, because we are invited to see him as lower than ourselves (whatever the truth, it is flattering and pleasurable for us to think so) and as an object of humor and ridicule, his violation of the social rules is not dangerous to our moral formation or to the social fabric. Nothing greater can be expected from such a fellow. Thus we are invited simultaneously to look down, as we laugh at him, and at the same time to watch his behavior closely and, if so inclined, to enjoy and even to identify with him. Consistency is not required in either the tragic or comic experience—that is why we find them comparatively easy to enjoy. We are not required to occupy a fixed point of view and stay with it; on the contrary, we may move about as the impulse or mood strike us. All that is required is that we admit to and follow our spontaneous feelings, even if they follow each other capriciously and contrary to all logic. If the comic gambit is successful, because we share his resentment, we will take an interest in the protagonist and follow his antics and rebellion with attention and curiosity. In fact, a part of us secretly will identify with him. We hope that his escapade somehow succeeds. We root him on, for part of us is riding with him. To use an expression from the Watergate era, we become "unindicted co-conspirators" in his low-grade mutiny. We want him to be happy because he is like us, and we want ourselves to be happy as well. As in Aristotle's theory of friendship, the potential opposition between egoism and altruism is taken away, resolved in the vision of a single object—a single personality—seen in two distinct places. By extracting this minor admission—that a part of ourselves has on occasion felt the same irritating constraint that the protagonist feels—the playwright has obtained all he wants from us, and all that he needs for his drama to succeed. At the first hint of a knowing smile on our lips, the battle is over, and he has won. The playwright has breached our defenses, stifled our boredom, and overcome our suspicion. We move into a mood of simultaneous relaxation and heightened anticipation. We like this fellow; we are intrigued with the story. We will stay with the action now to the end to see how it comes out.

As the house lights dim, no one is able to see what delight we might be taking in his outrageous escapades. There is a guarantee of complete anonymity in the theater. We are granted, if you will, the release of confession, that is, of acknowledging, at least to ourselves, the resentment or pent-up feelings we have long felt. This admission is exacted from us by humor, by our knowing laughter, which is based upon an admission that, yes, on occasion I *have* found these rules burdensome and unneeded, I *have* felt like doing just what the protagonist is doing. If we are going to get any enjoyment at all out of the situation, we must first make such an admission. Through the comic protagonist I am lured into acknowledging a side to myself which I ordinarily keep hidden, perhaps even from myself. Several circumstances conspire to induce this change of attitude. First, as mentioned, the theater is a special, protected environment, and thus nonthreatening. The darkness produces a sense of protective anonymity. No one can see who is laughing, no one will be at the door taking our names as we leave. When you think about it, this whole experience is a type of agreed-upon self-deception or group charade; it is something we are all going through at the same time, but we are all doing it individually and separately. Further, no one knows how the other parties are reacting. At the end, if you like, you do not have to admit how much you enjoyed it. You may assume a stuffy, proper bourgeois attitude and claim that, actually, you found the whole affair dreadfully tedious, even if during it you hid your face in your hand from laughing. Honesty is not demanded. Hypocrisy is fully licensed and is even encouraged. All that is required is that you have a good time. But the price of getting out of the theater having enjoyed yourself is that you first make this one small confession: you know how the comic hero feels, you know what he is going through. You have already put down money and given up time to be there; you might as well make this last small concession, and thereby save the entire evening from being a wash-out and complete waste of time.

In the course of his rebellion, the comic protagonist typically receives a mild correction or comeuppance as the price for his antisocial behavior. Through this penalty he undergoes a "conversion" or turning back toward the norm he initially flouts. The consequences of violating this norm are brought home to him concretely, if not too painfully, and their ultimate rationality is thereby revealed and impressed upon him. At the end there is typically a reconciliation with the social norm, a closing of the gap or discrepancy initially opened up between the individual and society's convention. Through our identification with the hero, we in the audience experience vicariously the penalty, and also, through the penalty, the conversion and final reconciliation as well. In the course of the evening, the audience may thus savor two distinct—and usually antithetical—pleasures: first, the thrill and joy of rebelling against the social norm, and later the satisfaction of seeing the wisdom behind the norm revealed, and of being reconciled with the convention. To us is given the knowledge of why the norm is the way it is, and we are reconciled to it not only at the intellectual, but also and more importantly, at the affective level, which is more difficult. Thanks to this comic drama, we have had the opportunity to experience, albeit vicariously, the alternative. Some pain results, but behind the pain the deeper appeal is to our reason. We accept the experience and the lesson gratefully, because we are being treated gently, as befits our adult status, and not like children who need to be punished severely.

We are protected from the more intense forms of suffering by several devices. As with tragedy, the playwright uses the various pleasures associated with exotic location, unusual and exalted language, colorful spectacle, music, and most crucially, a unified plot, with a clear beginning, middle, and end—unlike our life, where so many things half start and half stop—as "perks" to charm, dazzle, distract, and in general to cushion the suffering associated with the conversion we must go through. The most effective device, that basic to all drama, is that the story is happening to someone *else*. The comic protagonist is our stand-in, our representative in the rebellion. When he is caught, he conveniently also becomes our representative in the punishment. We can, if we like, deny all knowledge of or sympathy with him at this point; he becomes in effect our whipping boy. This is unfair, of course, even a form of exploitation; but then, who ever said we were coming to the theater to be *fair?* We take advantage of the situation, even pay handsomely for it, find it a great relief, and enjoy it immensely on several levels. Comedy is a transaction between consenting adults, after all; both sides know what is going on and agree voluntarily to the conditions of the exchange.

This vicarious punishment is so much better than being corrected ourselves. When it is done this way, we are still corrected, but the punishment is so modified and indirect, we almost do not feel it. We get the best of both worlds: the rebellion, the lesson, and the correction without the pain. This version of punishment, if not a vice, is

certainly a luxury, one to which we enjoy becoming accustomed. We wish all our correction could be done this
gently. Our motive for enjoying comedy, one notices, is
not necessarily the highest or most noble. This does not
mean that comedy isn't good for us. It simply means that
we are constitutionally weak and self-pitying creatures,
given to seeking the easiest and least difficult way for
ourselves, and that comedy accommodates this condition
to a considerable degree. Deep down, we seem to recognize intuitively that we need correction—we even *want* to
be corrected—but we want it to be done gently. Comedy,
we discover perhaps to our surprise, is the mildest form of
correction available. As we mature our tastes change; we
need less "shock" to elicit the same result from us. We
cherish a genre that ministers to our metaphysical weakness while recognizing us for the mature, sophisticated,
and flexible adults we like to think we are. As we grow in
experience, we see beyond the laughter of comedy to
recognize this aspect of correction in the comic experience, and are drawn to it at this level precisely because of
the relatively painless insight, correction, and possibility
of conversion it makes available. Within this unusual
kind of social upbraiding,[1] we are initially allowed the joy
of complicity in a rebellion (which is a painless form of
confession), and subsequently the pleasure of seeing the
ultimate wisdom behind the norms we first found so
burdensome—and forgiveness for the rebellion is virtually guaranteed! It is an unbeatable deal.

Comedy induces our identification and achieves this
manipulation in a straightforward and rather unsubtle
fashion. When you want someone to do something, it is a
common psychological trick to give him two options: the
one you want him to choose, and another that is worse or
more difficult. That way the person chooses the one you
want him to anyway, and also thinks that it is his own
idea, and that he is doing it freely. You allow him a
modest victory—his own autonomy—as the price for get-

ting him to do what *you* want him to. He is able to salvage a bit of pride from the situation; that way it is not a complete humiliation. Comedy frequently seems to use the same device. A comedy will typically present us with two sorts of characters: in Aristotle's terms, a vicious person, who is already set in his evil ways; and a "weak-willed" person, that is, a person who has had a proper formation, but who is now being tempted, is wavering, and is flirting with the possibility of adopting the life style of the vicious. Given this choice, most people spontaneously identify with the weak-willed person as the more attractive (or less unattractive) of the two. The comic hero is this weak-willed person, and he is being tempted to rebel against the social norms. If his rebellion becomes permanent or hardened, he is in danger of becoming vicious himself. However, he is as yet still "plastic" or malleable; there is yet a chance for correction and redemption. The iron pull of habit has not hardened these rebellious acts into an unbreakable "second nature" that merits severe punishment. As the story progresses, some of the vicious people surrounding the protagonist typically suffer the penalty their conduct deserves, thus acting as a lesson to those of us (the hero *and* the audience) who are only "weak-willed." The comic hero himself comes close to becoming vicious and suffering the same fate. At the last minute, however, as he sees their fate, he is frightened, sees the reason behind the norm, and steps back. He (and through him, we) are "scared straight," and are thereby reconciled to the social norm from which we have at first rebelled.[2]

Comedy thus builds upon and exploits this hope in a moral universe and this agreement with fate we have unconsciously made. When we do something wrong, we do want to be corrected, but corrected gently—as people who are fundamentally good and who have only gone astray, not as people who have become vicious. You see, we seem to say, this evil deed does not really indicate my

true self or reveal my true condition, nor does it alter my
fundamentally good orientation. In short, it is not an
accurate indication of who I really am. You see, I am not
one of the vicious people, but only morally weak. In our
own minds all of us naturally place ourselves among the
"good people" of the world. For one thing, we each have
special access to our own "inner goodness"—which no-
body else can see. Other people have to judge by our
external behavior. "Fate has not been kind to me," I seem
to say, "I have not gotten what I deserve; that is why I
occasionally do the things I do." There is every sort of
excuse and extenuating circumstance. Most of us, it
seems, are permanently ready to wallow in self-pity. We
want others to see us as we see ourselves and to agree with
our relaxed and forgiving evaluation of ourselves. We
want to be corrected as fundamentally good people who
have only lost their way, and not as willfully evil. This
preferred way of seeing ourselves is well captured in the
plaintive appeal of the "Whiffenpoof Song":

> To the tables down at Mory's
> To the place where Louis dwells,
> To the dear old Temple Bar we love so well,
> Sing the Whiffenpoofs, assembled
> With their glasses raised on high,
> And the magic of their singing casts its spell.
> . . . .
> We will serenade our Louis
> While life and voice shall last,
> Then we'll pass and be forgotten with the rest.
>
> We're poor little lambs who have lost our way,
> Baa! Baa! Baa!
> We're little black sheep who have gone astray;
> Baa! Baa! Baa!
> We are gentlemen songsters off on a spree,
> Doomed from here to eternity;

Lord have mercy on such as we:
Baa! Baa! Baa![3]

There is sadness and self-pity behind the surface gaiety and nostalgia of this drinking song. Similarly, in the dynamics of comedy, we are conscious of our faults, of how far we fall short of the ideal or what we should be, but we beg to be treated gently and with mercy—as weak-willed, and not vicious people deserve. Most people spontaneously place themselves in this category, no matter how long-standing their bad habits may be. They find the comic protagonist attractive or nonthreatening on this account, easier and more natural to identify with than the vicious people. In effect, we are allowed to confess and plead guilty to the lesser of two charges, in the moral "plea-bargaining" offered to us by the playwright. Comedy plays upon this human tendency toward self-leniency, it accommodates and acquiesces compassionately in our relaxed appreciation of our own moral condition. In effect, comedy combines the release of confession with the guarantee of forgiveness and with the mildest of punishments; it is the best deal we can strike. We recognize it as such; we gravitate towards it; we take it; and we change as best we can. In our heart of hearts, in our deepest imaginations, we are all of us fighting on the side of the angels, in the cause of truth and right. Comedy gives us the chance to say that—and thus, perhaps, to make it true. Somehow, such things, until they are said (like marriage vows), are not really true, or perhaps not yet true. The data is ambiguous or underdetermined; it could be interpreted in alternative ways. The playwright, like God, agrees to look upon that part of ourselves that *we* want to highlight, and to ignore the rest, or to accept our interpretation of the situation; and perhaps we will change. The recognition of our faults is no guarantee, but it is the first, essential step to such a conversion; and that, after all, is the point and secret agenda of the whole transaction. Comedy is a partial charade carried out between consenting adults. The comic author does not have to win his full thesis about our past lives, if he can succeed in getting us to make a partial confession and to agree to modifying our future actions; and we do not have to be declared *totally* innocent, if we are allowed to plead guilty to a lesser charge than the data perhaps suggest, and promise to amend. That way both sides get what they want. Each side backs down from its initial demand and compromises; a deal is struck. We react to the comic author the same way we react to God. He offers us forgiveness. We accept his offer. The past, whatever it is, is wiped away; and we promise to amend.

Of course, the comic hero is only an actor. There is really no suffering going on; it is all pretend or make-believe. But by the magic of drama, the psychological effect is similar to what happens when it *is* real. The amazing property about imitation, about dramatic art, involving the "willing suspension of disbelief," is that the line between reality and illusion blurs. We cease to attend to the fact that what we are seeing is only make-believe. We react to it as if it *were* real. The same biological flight-or-fight mechanisms, the same emotions of anger, fear, love, and hate are aroused as they would be in real life, only in a modulated or attenuated form.[4] The great discovery about drama is that it has the ability to concentrate, encapsulate, and speed up experience in such a way that it saves us the trouble of going through it ourselves, which is a great boon to us for the more terrible forms of experience. In comedy, we enter enough into the emotional state of the protagonist to enjoy his rebellion, but *also* to be shocked, chastised, and corrected by his later, and deserved, ill fortune. We ride parasitical and piggyback upon his experience; a slap to him is also a (modulated) slap to us. Through the magic of drama, his lesson serves to benefit us as well, and through the protagonist's experiences, we catch a glimpse of our own fate, if we act on our disruptive impulses or persist in our antisocial tendencies.

In classical comedy it is typically the individual who recognizes that he is wrong, that his rebellion was a mistake, and who "converts" to reaccept the social norm. However, reconciliation may take place in other ways as well. In modern comedy, increasingly it is the social norm which is judged to be inadequate and which, in the final reconciliation, must be modified and structurally altered to conform to the individual's needs. This is the "Copernican Revolution" which has taken place in modern drama, as well as in modern philosophy. At its extreme, this development can lead comedy into the neighboring (and respectable) genre of propaganda. This ethos is found in the modern comic novel, for example, where there is frequently behind the humor a smarting wound, some barely suppressed anger, and possibly a practical or reform agenda against perceived outdated or unjust social structures. Such an intention is already apparent in *Don Quixote*, where the protagonist is held up for ridicule as some one living according to anachronistic social conventions, and more clearly in Fielding's *Tom Jones*. Tom is presented as "innocent," guileless, or basically good. The social structures and institutions which should be supporting him are actually exploiting and oppressing him, but Tom does not see this, and the narrator similarly describes them in traditional exalted or "mock-heroic" language. As with Huck Finn's innocent but realistic descriptions of what he experiences along the river, the gap between what he says and what the reader is allowed to see produces a sense of irony, a detached (and humorous) appreciation of how far men's actions or the conditions of society are falling short of what they should be. When this gap is pressed further, the aesthetic experience and the resulting knowledge are sometimes intended by the author to prod the audience into action to change society's institutions. Most of Berthold Brecht's plays fall into this category. The energy aroused during the drama is not intended to be resolved *within* the play itself, but rather to survive and spill over outside it. Here, indeed, a "fine art" is close to becoming a "practical" or utilitarian art in the literal sense.

Occasionally, the discrepancy between the individual and society, or between the actual and the ideal, can become so complete that it apparently cannot be crossed; the gap then cannot be closed. In this case, action no longer seems a viable or practical response, for no reconciliation is possible; by default, we must fall back to contemplation. When comedy becomes contemplative or theoretical in this sense, it typically also becomes black or pessimistic. We have few if any examples of this from the ancient or medieval periods; it seems a distinctively modern development. One thinks of the humor in such novels as Joseph Heller's *Catch 22*. Laughter becomes all that we can do, all that is left to us, but the insight we discover at the base of the humor is no longer oriented to changing either ourselves or the situation. We initially laugh at the discrepancies and unexpected juxtapositions presented, but then we catch sight of the skull leering at us from behind the flowers, and our mirthful mood is spoiled. We laugh initially because we are nervous in such surroundings as suffering and death, and there is nothing else we can do. Then we realize the horror we are laughing at, and this insight chokes our merriment. The pessimism behind this form of comedy becomes apparent. It is more profound and complete, as Walter Kaufmann notes, than that of tragedy, for tragedy at least believes in the (possible) nobility of human beings, no matter what the rest of the cosmos (including the gods) may be like (T&P, 349). Contemplative or theoretical comedy has lost even that.

In conclusion, we may say that in comedy as well as in tragedy, there is a "catharsis," or purging of emotions. But the emotions that have been aroused and to some degree indulged are our boredom, our antisocial feelings, and our resentment at norms and rules which at times seem to do violence to our true feelings. The artistry of the playwright allows us to be diverted and entertained, awakening and playing upon our craving for the strange, the unusual, the exotic, the forbidden, the out of bounds—not by leading us into fantasy, bad taste, or depravity where we otherwise might have to go in search of them, but paradoxically, by leading us back *toward* the commonplace, everyday realities, and even toward the social norms—and allowing us to see them as fresh and even innovative possibilities. It is no wonder George Meredith has called comedy "the great civilizer." It is indeed a minor miracle. It is also the least painful form of confession, correction, and moral learning available. Whatever its initial intent or lowly origin in diatribe and invective, this is the surprising social task comedy was discovered to be uniquely empowered to carry out. Comedy is useful for the stabilization of society, and serves as a tonic and aid for the return of the individual to moral virtue. It is certainly one of the blessings of civilization, hardly a luxury but a necessity for an adult population, and a precious antidote for our (permanent) metaphysical weakness. It is a kind of secular sacrament, spontaneously developed and intuitively reached for, virtually a gift from the gods extended perhaps out of compassion and compensation to minister to our derivative, creaturely condition. When we are bitter, resentful, lethargic, or depressed, comedy is the great nurturer and the great restorer. It can set us back on our feet and give us new lease on life—on practical life, where the majority of our living must take place. It is the female of the dramatic genres, it calls forth or represents the female side to our personality, reconciling us to the routine but necessary side of existence, which we sometimes find unacceptably boring. Tragedy deals with the masculine side, that of risk and achievement, which we also long for *and* simultaneously shrink from. Both get us over the "hump" of resistance to what must be done. Comedy declines to address the mountain peaks of life, leaving them to tragedy; its concern is more modestly to shore up the "platform" of life without which no high points can be attempted. Comedy allows us to carry on our social existence with verve and renewed confidence. As contemplation cannot get by, or even get started, without practical virtue, tragedy cannot be attempted except by a society brought back to earth and made secure by comedy. If tragedy awakens us to our higher possibilities, comedy reminds us of, and forces us to address, our lower necessities. We need both to get by, as each ministers to a different side of our mixed condition. Of the two, tragedy is perhaps more the luxury in the sense that it is the more dispensable. Comedy is the more necessary. Tragedy is a production of luxury and leisure, whereas comedy is essential for producing the leisure required to attempt tragedy. In a society without tragedy, comedy would still have to be written. Without comedy, neither tragedy, nor life itself, would long be possible.

4
Raising the Pucker Factor

Like the comic playwright, the tragic playwright must fulfill the basic contract of delivering pleasure. Presumably, a "tragedy" is going to tell us a sad or disturbing story, or bring us bad news, so how does the playwright bring us pleasure along the way? How can he induce us to stay with the story? What kind of pleasure can he offer us?

The first and distinctive pleasure in tragedy is rather obvious. It is the inducement to identify with the hero, and it is a transparent appeal to our pride. Whereas comedy presents us with a person a bit below the average, and invites us to a "moral holiday," as William James calls it, a vicarious freedom from inhibition and the release of confession, tragedy presents us with a person a bit above the average (at least), and appeals directly to our vanity. It is clear that neither comedy nor tragedy tap elevated motives in their audience. If they did, they would not be as successful as they are at ensnaring us. The miracle is that they deliver a satisfaction in excess, both in quality and quantity, of what they at first promise, where the unavoidable pain involved in our "conversion" becomes surprisingly a part of the subsequent pleasure. The delight is that the playwright discovers and pushes us toward our better selves, after having seduced us by appealing to our lower selves. We are grateful, because entertainment often does the reverse: we are made to laugh at things we would just as soon not laugh at. Our metaphysical weakness, our craving for diversion, is exploited to our own disadvantage and metaphysical damage or impairment. Here the opposite takes place: we leave the theater better than we came in. The contract has been fulfilled in a way we did not anticipate, we are intrigued and richly satisfied, and consequently we reward the playwright handsomely. He has done more than entertain us—he has restored us to the selves we always knew we were, or at least wanted to be. We are grateful for his faith in us—more faith, perhaps, than we had in ourselves—and for lifting us up to what we knew we should be.

To return to the chief pleasure in tragedy, the entrance of an impressive, perhaps even a magnificent human being sparks our interest and arouses our admiration. Our self-image is flattered by the mere introduction of such a person, and also by the implicit invitation to compare ourselves with him, perhaps even to identify vicariously with a person who is obviously above average, probably splendid and stunning. It is impossible to be indifferent in the presence of such a spectacle, and difficult to decline such an invitation. For one thing, the inevitable comparison challenges our sense of our own worth. Admiration mixes with envy and rivalry as we feel ourselves rising to this new and sudden challenge. Also the Walter Mitty in each one of us comes out. He may be magnificent, but after all, he is not all that different from me. He is king of Thebes. Well, in different circumstances, *I* could be king of Thebes as well. True or not, few of us can decline or back down from such a provocation. Thus, besides the flattery, our spirit of competition pushes us to compare and identify with him since I am persuaded that I am already like him—at least in my own imagination.

A new motive strengthens the initial admiration and comparison for we know that, in the play, bad things will soon happen to the protagonist. How will he weather the coming storm? Perhaps we have seen the play before, and know exactly what the lines are, so that in a sense we know how he is supposed to react. Still, how will this actor *show* him encountering these adversities? Our interest is piqued; we begin to pay closer attention. Our initial admiration and identification blend into a subsequent mixture of perhaps less commendable motives. He thinks he is so great; well, let's see how great he *really* is. Will he hold up? We want to see. There is an unmistakable voyeuristic streak, a mordant and morbid curiosity blended into our admiration for the protagonist. We are pulled in opposing directions of admiration and envy. Implicit in the latter is a certain amount of self-pity as well. If he is such a great man, and bad things are going to happen to him—well, my life has been no bowl of cherries either. In fact, we have here another basis for comparison and identification, for life has been unfair to me as well. These two factors mix to strengthen our curiosity and to attach us more firmly to the plot. We will stay with the action to the end. We want to see *how* he suffers. We want to see if he's as strong as he thinks he is. We dislike anybody being better than we are, and if we can't rise to his level, we prefer at least to pull him down to our own. The clever tragic author exploits these perhaps less noble or commendable psychological impulses to achieve his own effect.

The tragic hero must have a high regard for himself. According to Aristotle this is not a vice, but a virtue. A deferential humility on the part of a great man is out of place and unbecoming, because emotions and regard should be proportional to a person's objective merit; and by definition a "great" man is worth more, is objectively better or more fully realized than others. If a great man has a low regard for himself, his friends will interpret that as a signal that he knows something about himself he is not showing, and that his "greatness" may be a charade. The great man *must* have a high regard for himself, and he expects others, of his own rank especially, to have a similar high regard for him as well. Aristotle is an unblushing elitist. We have to get used to this difference to our modern egalitarian bias, which both he and Plato would find puzzling, nontraditional, and nonempirical. For them, there are obviously better and worse types of human being. These are not to be identified simply along lines of class or wealth, but Aristotle admits that it is hard to practice certain virtues, as well as to lead a happy life, if you are poor. Further, both would agree that society's structures should be oriented toward producing and sustaining the best kinds of human beings. That is why, for Aristotle, in a friendship between unequals, the lower owes the higher more, for he is worth more (1158b 25–29), and reciprocally, the higher cannot and should not take as much interest in the lower, because the latter is worth less. That is also why God cannot take an interest in or even know about the world, as he is appropriately taken up with himself, the highest object in the universe. Because the gap between them is so wide, a reciprocal relationship between God and man is ruled out as impossible (1159a5).

Suffering is an act that, like other acts for Aristotle, can be done well or badly. Great men are expected to suffer "well" or "greatly." What does this mean? Basically, it means that he must keep his self-command and sense of personal worth even under physical and psychological torment. He must not accept his tormentors' or inferiors' view of him. Like Sophocles's Philoctetes, he may cry out in pain all he wants. The fact of his misfortune should perhaps induce him to examine himself to see if he has done something that makes justifiable what is happening to him, but if he decides that he has not, then he must not, under the strain of physical torture, break down, alter his fundamental self-estimate, or begin to grovel before his tormentors. He may ask to be killed by a single blow or in a dignified manner, if die he must, as his station and character merit; to have one's tortures protracted and to be exposed to mockery is a death appropriate to a slave or a criminal, both of which he is convinced he is not, but he should not lose his dignity or suffer a change in character. Having reviewed the situation and decided that he is not guilty, he must still not be afraid to die. He must not grovel before his inferiors simply because they have the power to grant his life. Life below a certain level should not have that much attraction for him, and pain should not have excessive power over him (1124b7). We are reminded of certain American Indian tribes where warriors captured from other tribes were expected, by both sides, to suffer well, that is, impassively, proudly, without showing cowardice, as a mark of pride for their clans. We know, of course, that such behavior is difficult to execute. We sit up and begin to watch the hero more closely. The ability to suffer this way, although in a sense expected, is still rare, and requires great courage and self-control. If it can be carried out, this display automatically arouses awe and calls forth our admiration.

This point may be broadened into a second basis for attention besides the flattery involved in the identification with such an impressive human being. When and if an unjust misfortune should strike him, the protagonist should not fall into the conventionally pious or orthodox response—he should show more strength and resolve than that. He should dare to follow his convictions, and not be frightened out of them by the prospect of total destruction. When a person shows such a courageous response, he automatically triggers both our anxiety and our interest, and he makes a further claim upon our attention. Specifically, the protagonist must not attempt to save the good name of the gods, their supposedly "Olympian" or "Apollonian" qualities, in the face of manifestly unjust or cruel treatment at their hands. He must not capitulate or be seen to grovel before the gods for the same reason he must not grovel before inferior men, merely because they are more powerful than he or may destroy him. He must not be cowed into assuming guilt for the situation merely to save the gods' good reputation or out of fear of offending them further. Rather, he must be faithful to what he sees and to his convictions about himself, he must not be intimidated but rather be ready to defy the gods, if need be, to throw responsibility for the situation back where it belongs, on their shoulders. If he makes the conventionally pious response, then he is in no way out of the ordinary, and he appears to have simply caved in before patently unjust, bullying treatment, as most men do most of the time. Whether he is right or wrong, such an act of defiance is dramatically powerful, and it calls out our respect and arouses our attention still further.

We may test this psychological criterion for interest or admiration by examining our response to other forms of literature where this same dynamic takes place or analogous issues are at stake. If we turn to the Book of Job, for example, I submit that an analogous opposition or contest is taking place, and that our response is similar. The Book of Job is sometimes taken as inculcating patience and perseverance in the face of repeated calamities. That may have been the point of the final editor, but if we examine Job's speeches to his three "comfortors" and to Elihu, and even to God, we will see that Job's behavior is quite different, and that our response and admiration for Job are based on the same character traits we have just mentioned.

The Book of Job belongs to a genre common to Near Eastern peoples called "wisdom literature." Wisdom literature began as a series of instructions from a scribe or court official to his students based on the principle that prosperity comes to the person who is wise; its deeper communication is that God is rational and benign, and that he rewards with prosperity the person who cultivates his own reason, gives God respect and worship, and is not troubled by temporary setbacks or difficulties. The man who maintains piety and holiness, who works hard, who does not murmur or do evil, will rise in the service of the king and also enjoy the blessings of God. Thus, the first lesson of wisdom literature is the unspoken agreement with fate we have mentioned above, which is also crucial to our enjoyment of comedy. Perhaps our desire to control and ensure our future is the reason people are drawn to both genres—to wisdom literature and to comedy. We want good things to happen to good people, and to get good things, we resolve to become good people.

As it developed, however, wisdom literature ultimately had to take account of counterdata to give its adherents the intellectual and psychological resources to deal with contrary or refractory sorts of experience, so that they would not fall into confusion, distress, and despair should calamities befall them. Good things do not always happen to good people. This later message is thus also a type of "wisdom," but now a kind modifying, if not directly contradicting, the first type. Thus, within the genre of wisdom literature, there developed a second and somewhat contrary movement. Although apparently opposed in thesis to the first, it is continuous with its general program of giving its followers an intellectual vision and the psychological strength to withstand the vicissitudes of fortune without serious turmoil, confusion, or pain. By "wisdom," therefore, they mean what Aristotle calls "practical wisdom" or prudence, that is, a skill built up rationally from experience as to how to survive and prosper during all sorts of circumstances, which is also what comedy aims at. The thrust of comedy is to inculcate and reinforce this "optimistic" thesis of early wisdom literature. But life isn't always like that. The thrust of tragedy is clearly to challenge and oppose this optimistic outlook. We welcome and can apparently enjoy both, for each shows us a different side or gives us a different angle of vision upon the same reality—our life—which remains mysterious, never fully transparent, perpetually refractory, something which certainly cannot be reduced to a single formula. To survive, we have to be prepared continually for contradictory sides of experience, and we need reminders and counsel for both. As said, the thesis of this second moment of wisdom literature is a modification or correction of its first thesis, so much so that it is sometimes referred to as "anti-wisdom." It is represented in our Bible by the Books of Job and Qoheleth, or Ecclesiastes.

Whatever the original story, the Book of Job may have been built up, modified, and retained more as a cautionary tale about what *not* to expect from fortune, with Job presented not so much as an example of perseverance and patience, but of challenge and refusal to accept blandly the wisdom thesis maintaining the parallel of virtue and happiness. To explain the power and continuing interest of this story, I suggest, this same curiosity in watching to see if the great man can "suffer well" must be recognized and taken into consideration.

Like many books in the Old Testament, the book is drawn from several sources, finally stitched together in the form we have it probably around the sixth century, B.C.E. Job is not even identified as a Hebrew. The beginning and the ending were probably originally separate from the set of speeches of Job with his three "comfortors" and with Elihu. Whether or not the book is finally meant to inculcate the wisdom thesis (which is disputed), our interest here is in the question of where the figure of Job derives his power and dramatic attraction. Whatever the intention of the authors, the effect of the story as it has come down to us is certainly to make us ponder and reflect on the plight of the good man struck down suddenly and apparently for no reason, and reduced to desperation by fortune. We in the audience have several options, as does Job. We may attempt to salvage an "optimistic" theology by suggesting that God tries the good person, or at least allows him to be tested, or we may move to the "blasphemous" or "unthinkable" theology that Ricoeur has described. Whatever our interpretation, the drama of the Book of Job is clearly close to that of tragedy, where the alarming proposal is also put forward implicitly that it is precisely the "great man" who becomes a lightning rod for the gods' attention, but that the gods' motives may not be as benign or rational as the biblical authors generally believe, but may rather represent the regressive theology that Ricoeur has described above; in short, the gods may not be good but evil. Tragedy forces us to confront the possibility that our unspoken compact with the gods is broken; there is no longer any connection between virtue and prosperity. Dare we face this vision?

Job is interesting against the backdrop of world literature in that, compared with other protagonists, he walks a tightrope, trying not to fall off in either of two directions. On the one hand, if we follow the wisdom thesis, if bad things happen to you, it must be as a punishment for something wrong you have done. Job's three friends come to "comfort" him, which really means they want to impose their view upon Job to get him to acknowledge that he has done something wrong—and thus to let God off the hook from the charge of being unjust. In other words, they do not so much want to comfort Job as they want themselves to be comforted, and their faith in their own rather too simplistic wisdom hypothesis to be reaffirmed and supported. It is they who are uncomfortable when this thesis is called into question, as it appears to be by the events in Job's life and the challenge that his subsequent refusal to accept guilt represents. Job listens to them, and does examine himself, but decides that their view is incorrect, that he has done nothing wrong, nothing at least that merits what he is receiving. At this point—and this is important, for it is not always noticed—Job refuses to buckle under the strain or give way. In particular he refuses to surrender his self-understanding and sense of self-worth. Like Jacob with the angel, he chooses rather to contend with God. Specifically, he refuses to assume guilt for the situation upon himself. He will not apologize or conclude that he has done something wrong. On the contrary, he challenges God to mention something wrong he has done. On the other hand—for the time being at least—he refuses to embrace the "blasphemous" theology that Ricoeur has described above as basic to tragedy. His wife does accept this dark point of view; she counsels Job to "curse God and die." In other words, God has you in his power. He is being unjust to you, torturing you for no good reason, but you can't do a thing about it for he is stronger than you. All that is left to you is to give him the defiant gesture his conduct merits, demonstrating that, even if you must die, you will not be cowed into denying your self worth, bullied or intimidated into saying something that is untrue, merely to avoid raising his anger further. If die you must, resolve at least to go out like a lion rather than like a goat, with your nobility and conscience intact. This is the tragic courage and response to unjust treatment, and we admire instinctively any protagonist who can muster such integrity and personal constancy, who can rise to such conduct in the face of great personal danger and risk.

Job refuses to do this as well. He will not curse God—not yet. But he makes it uncomfortable for those who would defend God, by deliberately leaving the issue hanging fire. It is for God to speak. This silence by Job, this refusal to accept responsibility for the situation, to plead for pardon for imaginary sins, frightens and appalls his friends, for by not accepting guilt for the situation, he inevitably points the finger at God, and implicitly indicts God as the source of the evil. This blasphemous theology makes them quake. By his refusal to speak, Job throws the weight of the situation back on God's shoulders. It is God who must give answer; it is God, and not Job, who has done this and has some explaining to do. At the same time Job holds back from pronouncing judgment or embracing a blasphemous theology, even though much of the data seem to point unambiguously in that direction. He can afford to "wait," in both senses: to let the issue hang fire, let the data speak for themselves; and to wait upon God as in his court, in his traditional role as an upright and innocent man. The two roles are not incompatible. This is what makes Job different from the tragic protagonist; his conversion to an "unthinkable" theology is not complete. On the other hand he still does not buckle or grovel. Rather he sets his face like flint, and by his very silence he throws the ball back into God's court. "Se hace cara de Indio" ("He makes the impassive face of an Indian") as the Spaniards remarked about the impressive powers of not showing any emotion they found in the indigenous people of this hemisphere. If Job must die, he will die with his pride, not having confessed to something he never did. We watch with interest and some amazement. This is what makes him an intriguing, "in-between" figure, and saves our admiration for him. In the dialogue we observe Job walking carefully a middle path he charts out for himself, satisfying neither rival group that is trying to attach him to itself. Their dissatisfaction, he seems to say, is their own problem. Against his wife, Job takes the role of partial advocate for God, making excuses, postponing making a negative judgment. Against his friends, he takes the role *against* God, or against at least their view of God. Job reserves and leaves open the possibility that God may have an inscrutable plan, his own hidden reasons for the disaster that is befalling him. God has been faithful in the past, and Job will not break faith with him now prematurely. God may have his own reasons for what is happening, which may be revealed later. In great pain, and manifesting enormous psychological strength, Job gives God the benefit of the doubt—for the time being. But we should not miss the fact that, although in a sense submissive, Job has turned the tables on God. It is Job who will be watching and judging God, not God who will be judging Job.[1] It is now God who is in the dock; it is he who must give an account and a justification for his actions. Job finds a way to save both his manhood *and* his faith. He refuses to curse God, but he refuses also to prostrate himself and grovel before him for crimes he has never committed. We never lose our interest in and respect for Job, as we do for his "comfortors." Our interest in him is not simply as a "blameless and upright" man, as he is described in the beginning of the story, but as the courageous man of enormously greater psychic strength he grows into and reveals himself to be as the story progresses. Like the tragic hero, Job increases in stature and grows in our admiration. He manifests new powers and virtues as the drama unfolds, and he is tested in new ways. Like the tragic hero, he "suffers well."

As we attend to a tragedy, similar questions circulate through our consciousness. How well will the protagonist suffer? Will he be able to bear the strain? Will he emerge as "great" from the suffering as he went into it, or will he cave in and reveal himself to be a weak man after all? Could *I* suffer as well? Would I crumble under the pressure? Would I be able to hold out as long as he does? Will the protagonist lose his self-possession, his nobility, and be reduced to a quivering mass of gelatin begging for his life? Will they break his nerve? Does he have the courage to refuse to accept the guilt for the situation, the dare to throw this implicit charge upon himself back into the gods' faces—to make it a charge against *them*? Can he *live* with this act of impiety, and take whatever punishment they choose to mete out to him for his act of defiance?

We in the audience catch on quickly to what is at stake and going on beneath the surface, and how much this implicit thesis is opposed to the conventional or orthodox point of view. We catch the scent; we don't have to be told twice. The poet has tapped into our deepest psychological images. He has dared to play out on the stage, and in public, a fantasy that, perhaps, has occurred to us privately, but which we personally have never had the courage to carry out, or perhaps even mention. Attractive and repulsive impulses play upon us simultaneously. The drama indulges our desire for rebellion from the familiar and routine, our craving for the novel and the unusual, with a vengeance. It takes advantage of this latent pool of psychological irritation to catapult us to where we would not otherwise choose to go. The beauty of the poetic language holds us in thrall by itself. We are in awe that such emotions dare to be named and expressed at all; it throws a dazzling and alluring veil of beauty over the basically unattractive and painful plot. This device makes bearable a fascinating and yet repulsive vision, as well as a steady, calm, and unwavering contemplation of something we may prefer to run away from. The artistic beauty of music, spectacle, and costume generates a countering positive attraction and insulating aesthetic screen which distances us from the immediate consequences of this event. Paradoxically it also moves the action into sharper focus, allowing us to attend to it steadily, not as the source of terror, but as an object of fascination, intrigue, and study. Again, unquestionably, a voyeuristic streak is awakened and engaged. It is to that same part of the soul that Plato refers in book four of the *Republic* as wanting to go running up and examine dead bodies, open wounds, and other repulsive but real aspects of our world. We are here given a unique opportunity to examine in detail a possibility whose presence we could not otherwise endure psychologically, but that we also would not normally get the chance to consider. We strain forward to watch the hero. We cannot take our eyes off him. We want to see how he reacts.

The consciousness of being in the presence of such a fundamental and serious blasphemy heightens both our anxiety and our attention to the situation. We sit transfixed and yet embarrassed to be present at all at such an unseemly conflict and cataclysmic struggle that, according to the canons of orthodoxy, should not be happening at all. It goes against our optimistic orthodoxy, the way we were told things should be, the idealistic outlook that is socially promulgated. We scramble to get out of the way in this contest between two powerful wills, neither of whom seems ready to back down or give way, and from which only one—if even one—can emerge intact. We seem to be thrown back and to have the same emotions as man the spectator in the primordial conflict between the gods in the Sumero–Babylonian creation drama. We really shouldn't be here at all. Further, this should not be going on. Perhaps if we close our eyes, it will go away.

Tragedy taps into and plays on long-forgotten memories, deeply buried family fantasies; it resurrects primeval archetypes which were the means by which we first cut up the world to understand it, and which underlie our interpretations even now. These images have a life of their own, and an on-going power to move and disturb us. The drama recalls, for example, our emotions when our older brother for the first time defied father. Such experiences and images carry a powerful emotional charge, and any situation which recalls them is fraught with anxiety for us, which only to some degree can be intellectualized and diffused. At such moments, we simultaneously wish this were not happening, that we could be anyplace else in the world but here. Yet we also would not leave this place for a moment, and we cannot take our eyes off it. We are terrified and yet curious to find out how it will come out. In a sense, we hate what we are seeing, for it really should not be happening. None of us should really be here, this whole thing should not be going on, let alone be depicted upon the stage. The whole drama is improper, an affront to the established orthodoxy and to official pieties. This cannot be good for any of us. And yet it is good for us, at least for those of us who cannot find any other way by which to handle this anxiety. We find that we cannot look away.

What we are seeing goes against everything we have been told; but perhaps what we were told was wrong. We decide that we will eat of the tree of knowledge of good and evil; we will judge what is good and evil for ourselves. We sit fascinated and perplexed. We are filled with a sense of dread or woe, and curiosity at the same time. Like children, we are tempted to bury our faces in our hands; but then we peek out from between our spread fingers. Time seems to stand still. Right now, nothing else in the universe seems as important as this. Our identity, or our way of conceiving ourselves and our condition, is being called into question. Will the hero be destroyed for his blasphemy? Is it possible to flout the gods with impunity? We pay rapt attention, and even take mental notes. Is it permissable to do what the hero is doing? Will the gods leave him unpunished? We watch for hints about our own past mistakes, and clues for future forms of more appropriate conduct. Either way, no matter how it comes out, whatever happens here will change our way of viewing ourselves and our world in the future, it will be determinative of a new self-understanding and behavior. There is no going back now to the way we were before. The hero is our stand-in, acting out our own imagined rebellion, volunteering to go first where we have not had the courage to go at all. He represents the next stage in our own development.

As with the comic hero, we participate vicariously in a rebellion against conventional orthodoxy through him. The tragic protagonist, however, has the grit to carry out a rebellion against not only social or practical conventions, but to call into question the most fundamental theoretical axioms on which society is built, the ones consequently surrounded and protected with the most powerful cultural, social, and religious taboos. His rebellion is consequently much more serious and terrifying. There is electricity in the air; dreadful anticipation sweeps through the audience and keeps our anxiety level high. This cannot go on forever—the strain is at times almost too great to bear.

The socially subversive aspect of the drama, the pleasure of acting out something forbidden in a clandestine manner, of being in a sense "naughty children" disobeying their parents, and the tingle associated with the danger of being surprised, arrested, and punished by outraged gods, or at the very least city fathers, contributes to our roiling cauldron of emotions and makes the situation deeply disturbing and yet intriguing. We will watch the hero closely now and follow the action to the end.

5
The Surprise Effect

This tragic blasphemy, this "unthinkable theology," accounts in large part for our attraction to and fascination with the tragic hero. It contributes substantially to the pleasure that is the reason we accept the initial invitation to identify with the protagonist and stay through the catastrophe to the end. The question I wish to address in this final chapter is the following: How might this tragic experience fit into, or even be compatible with, Aristotle's overall pattern of human development, since his crowning knowledge of metaphysics is admittedly nontragic, or even antitragic?

If comedy is oriented toward "practical knowledge," toward discerning the mean in things that can be changed, can tragedy be said to orient us toward theoretical or contemplative knowledge? It is tempting to think so, and Aristotle offers a few hints in that direction, although he never states it explicitly. It would make the justification for tragedy in an Aristotelian framework of human development clearer, and it would complete the parallel with comedy. Tragedy would orient us toward knowledge, but this time toward objects that cannot be changed or be other than they are—thus, objects of which *only* contemplative knowledge is possible. As comedy orients us to explore the relationships between the individual and society, tragedy would broaden the scope of our gaze significantly, to explore the relations between man and the cosmos as a whole—the gods or the fates. But there are some difficult questions to be answered before we proceed to make this assertion. First, how can the terrifying experience of tragedy be an aid to the construction of contemplative or theoretical knowledge? Second, why is it needed? After all, according to Aristotle all men naturally desire to know, and this kind of knowledge, of the highest speculative objects, should bring the purest, most divine type of pleasure. Shouldn't men progress to it naturally and inevitably, without the need for any outside stimulus or incentive? And third, of course, how can the experience of tragedy be an aid toward the construction of a nontragic (Aristotelian) metaphysic?

The progress in intellectual virtue is described by Aristotle as straightforward and unproblematic. As stated earlier, it involves working our way up through the various regional sciences toward an integrating or overarching form of knowledge—if such can be realized. However, there are so many local sciences, from shipbuilding to mathematics to music, that the project to find a finite and manageable set of categories that could integrate the whole of our knowledge might be unrealizable. Any such candidate set of ideas might be choked by the avalanche of different types of knowledge to be assimilated; the best we can produce might be an encyclopedia and not a system. Still, the project seemed worth attempting. Also, any such "highest science" would necessarily involve and allow us whatever partial glimpse is available to us of the highest substance in the universe, for this functions as the first cause of everything else. Only as organized under such a first cause can the variety and welter of objects of our experience be reduced to a unity, and thus become accessible to us for the first time as objects of a single study. Apparently the completion of intellectual virtue, then, or the construction of the highest theoretical science, requires us to raise the question of the gods.

As described by Aristotle, the person who has knowledge of an area is able to name the cause behind the fact to be explained, whereas the person who has belief knows only *that* something happens. The person who has knowledge is able to answer the question "why?" We convert our beliefs into knowledge or science, therefore, by discovering the causes behind the facts we observe. In the case of the regional or local sciences, the "facts" to be explained are clear and available to everyone. As we progress to the higher and more speculative objects, however, the "facts" or data become less accessible. These data consist in large part for Aristotle in the order and highest axioms of the former, subordinate sciences. He, like Plato, seems to assume that, because the gods are regular and unchangeable in their natures, a rigid, mathematical necessity will (and must) characterize the relations between the highest objects and those below (1139b13). An empiricist, but not with the modern sceptical attitude, Aristotle speaks of "intuitions" arising spontaneously, or "coming to stand" like soldiers running in a line when one stops, as we immerse ourselves in the data. Since the objects of this science are purportedly the highest causes in the universe, themselves uncaused, there is no way of knowing them through other objects higher than themselves. If they are to be known at all, we can only do so through objects lower than themselves (their effects), that we can experience directly, or perhaps *indirectly* through a kind of "rational intuition" on which Aristotle does not elaborate, but that he seems to imply comes from immersing and exposing ourselves repeatedly to the data (1141a 1–7). In fact, he has no hesitation in speaking about these highest axioms as being "intuitively clear" or "necessarily true," as if all researchers would naturally agree about them, since they concern objects that are "most knowable in themselves" or "most intelligible"—although initially, as mentioned earlier, Aristotle admits that we find them obscure and difficult to see due to the dimness of our eyes and their dazzling brightness.

It is at this point, in the highest axioms about the gods, that difficulties arise, both for the modern sceptical mind and for the empirical consciousness of all times. Ordinary mortals might ask, how can we get such a clear intuition about the gods? Aren't they closed off to our direct empirical inspection? How are we to test a statement someone makes about them? After all, we have plenty of myths about the gods already, and philosophy (for the Greek Enlightenment) began in large part precisely as the project to *cleanse* and correct these myths. Aristotle himself is quite critical of many of these stories. If these intuitions are so clear and distinct, so intuitively and necessarily true, then how is it that the authors of the past missed them? Or why should we now trust Aristotle over his predecessors?

Thus, there are reasons why it may be difficult to realize our formation in intellectual virtue, to complete the edifice of knowledge. It seems to get more difficult toward the last stage than it was at lower stages. The necessary intuitions seem to be lacking or difficult to attain in this thin, ethereal realm, and our resistance to certain unattractive or painful hypotheses about the gods may discourage us or make us disinclined to attempt such a study. There thus seems to be a "hump" we have to get over before that postulated "purest" pleasure can kick in and make the whole enterprise worthwhile; but unless we can get over this hump, our project to knowledge may become mired and stalled short of its goal, our natural desire to know the real remain permanently unsated, and the endeavor to think may become a partial and impeded activity, characterized by friction and incompleteness—thus a source of frustration and pain rather than our most satisfying and pleasurable activity, as it is supposed to be. How and when can we get an intuition that will acquaint us with a "cause" in this area, that will ground our beliefs and transform them into "knowledge"? Are we doomed to remain perpetually blind in this most important inquiry? That would be a cruel joke for the gods to play—to implant the desire but at the same time to withhold or render impossible the completion and satisfaction. We may well have reached an impasse in the project to knowledge; there is a serious possibility that this may be as far as we can go. That is the conclusion of the modern Enlightenment, for example, a position presented most explicitly and forcefully, perhaps, in the philosophy of Kant.

Can tragedy be relevant here? Could it come to our rescue or aid us in some way in this dilemma? Something like that seems implied in the suggestion that tragedy helps us toward theoretical or contemplative knowledge. Two things are needed at this point: first, a special energy to help us up and over this "hump," if we are not to become stalled or permanently bogged down. Second, we require some kind of "intuition," a powerful insight or analogous psychological experience that could be said to ground our belief and transform it into a form of defensible "knowledge." Our progress in the program of knowledge can apparently no longer be linear or cumulative as it has been up to this point. If we demand or wait for such an intuition according to past precedent, we will most likely become discouraged and give up the enterprise altogether. Nothing like that is to be expected, but perhaps we can make here a type of "progress" that involves examining critically our previous assumptions—not necessarily to reject them, but at least to become aware of alternatives, and thus possibly of reasons why we accept the ones we do—as in a Platonic dialectic, where the conclusions and method of one speaker are put into an altered or broader perspective by the next, to be relativized, if not directly opposed or contradicted, by the change in the context and angle of vision. (In the *Topics*, Bk. 1, Aristotle indicates that it is by dialectical reasoning, as distinct from inductive reasoning, that the axioms of the highest [contemplative] sciences are established.) We must then begin casting about and looking for unusual, untried, and perhaps counterintuitive avenues of investigation that might provide alternative experiences that could prove relevant to the dilemma, or *aporia*, in which we find ourselves. Perhaps it was Aristotle's unexpected discovery, and later his provocative suggestion, that tragedy could be one such experience, that it could provide both the energy to help us over the psychological difficulty, and also the intuitions to ground reasonably, if indirectly, our beliefs, which thus will allow us to keep ascending and perhaps even complete (insofar as this is available to us) the pyramid of contemplative knowledge and intellectual virtue.

I wish to agree with Kaufmann in his suggestion that tragedy gave the initial provocation, and may still function today, to propel people toward this type of speculative question that we all find difficult to face. Historically, I agree that it gave rise to what became known as "philosophy" (in the sense of a nontragic, rationally grounded worldview). Further, without tragedy, either as an aesthetic experience or in their personal lives, many people would not attend to these speculative questions at all and thus would not attain this level of theoretical penetration.

Tragedy may have been a necessary stimulus to turn the minds of the ancient authors to their unexamined assumptions and to whatever deficiencies, or at least meaningful alternatives, there might be in their philosophies—as painful as this kind of examination may be. Tragedy made them realize that they had to ground their first principles in at least a semblance of reason if they were to transform their nontragic beliefs into a defensible nontragic *knowledge*. The surprising or paradoxical result that Aristotle was perhaps the first to observe is that the existence and flowering of tragedy is not only compatible with the acceptance of a *nontragic* world view, but that tragedy may be an aid or even essential in producing the latter for some people, in the sense that only the sting or goad of the dreadful tragic experience is successful at rousing them from their "doxalogical" (or "belief") slumbers, to transpose Kant's phrase, and propelling them toward the difficult task of examining critically their received belief systems—mythic or otherwise—and seeing if they can possibly be transformed into a nontragic *knowledge* in whatever restricted or relaxed form we decide knowledge is available for us in this area.

Tragedy provided the stimulus, or perhaps the irritant, necessary to propel thinkers to this crucial (and never resolved) stage of the Greek Enlightenment. In this sense (as Kaufmann rightly claims), tragedy goes *beyond* the Greek Enlightenment as it is represented by Plato and Aristotle for it raises the question of the relation between God and the world, which these thinkers approached, but whose Parmenidean resources or assumptions did not allow them to resolve. This is not to say that we have to accept the opposing view—the blasphemous, irrationalist, tragic theology—but we have to confront it directly or head-on, and see the point it is making, before we make our decision.

If we are Parmenideans (as both Plato and Aristotle were), we cannot remain as we were before. Tragedy then becomes a shattering experience. We are in a state of theological innocence *before* we undergo a tragedy, a condition which we can never quite return to or recapture afterward. Tragedy plants deep seeds of suspicion; it provides a permanent theological nightmare and alternative in our psyche which refuses afterward to be dispelled by simply restating the old myths or repeating the Parmenidean assurances. These questions will hereafter not go away. They demand that we develop some new belief or philosophic system that has at least the appearance of handling them. On the broader scale of history, then, tragedy may indeed have been essential if our civilization was to make any further progress in enlightenment, or come to a higher maturation.

Aristotle did not have the resources to articulate a non-

Parmenidean response to the challenge of tragedy. He thus tried to smother or diffuse the challenge that a god was needed to produce the world by the simple device of declaring that the world had no beginning. Thus, it was the poverty of his own resources, rather than the experience of tragedy, that led him to the strategic modification that appears to us today as a confusing smokescreen, but ultimately as an inadequacy or serious *lacuna* in his program to give a complete explanation for the world (according to his paradigm of fourfold causality). But, was this decision by Aristotle to occupy a generic nontragic metaphysic simply a "cop out"? Was it necessarily an irrational backlash or failure of nerve before the experience of tragedy, as Kaufmann thinks that it was? Are there not other possibilities? Could it possibly have been a reflective response to this stimulus, resulting from a calm and attentive examination, fully conscious and deliberate, of the suggestion tragedy puts forward? We cannot rule this out *a priori*. This indeed is the central question to which our investigation has brought us: Could the experience of tragedy lead reasonably, even if paradoxically, to the acceptance of a *nontragic* worldview? More generally, whether we believe in special "rational intuitions" or not, is there *any* way to convert our nontragic belief systems, be they mythic or philosophic, into *knowledge* properly so called and defensible as such? And in particular, may tragedy function as a help in this process?

If tragedy could be an aid to developing contemplative knowledge about the highest substances, does it do this by supplying a new experience or direct intuition, which would acquaint us with this new "cause"? This is possible, but unlikely, difficult to maintain, and not essential. Perhaps if we relax our conditions of "knowledge," we can see how Aristotle might claim that tragedy does supply an indirect experience or analogue to such a causal intuition, one that can give a kind of assurance that would ground our claim and justify our move to a nontragic worldview, and claim that this move is not merely a knee-jerk reaction based on fear and irrational compulsion, but on the contrary a reasonable, conscious, and deliberate (if dialectical) transition. Kaufmann's criticism of Aristotle's motives reveals an incomplete appreciation of what we go through in attending a tragedy. Not only need Aristotle's response to tragedy *not* be based on fear and irrational impulse, but the claim might be made in fact that tragedy makes possible for the first time a nonfearful, noncompulsive response to the tragic vision. Aristotle himself tells us that in this highest and most speculative of all sciences, the science of "Being *qua* Being," we must fall back to a looser use of language, and hence be content with a more relaxed form of knowledge, for the term "Being" falls into equivocation, or several distinct meanings, which threaten the possibility of science or unified discourse in this area. Aristotle tells us this equivocation is significantly compromised, and knowledge thus salvaged from disintegrating into chaos, only by Being's primary reference to *one* object, the highest substance. Aristotle does not discuss how we can have direct contact with this invisible and unmoving first entity, so causal knowledge in the usual sense would seem to be ruled out in principle in this highest and most speculative area. As God tells Moses, no man sees God and lives. Well then, we might ask, is there any sense in which tragedy could supply an analogue or surrogate for causal knowledge of these objects?

To answer this question, we must consider the nature of our apprehensions concerning what may be called the classical or nontragic worldview, apprehensions that are perennial and constant in nature, but that have been heightened enormously in the modern period, especially since the work of Nietzsche and Freud. The ever-stronger suspicion has been that we accept this nontragic worldview, not as the result of a calm reflection and reasoned decision, but out of fear or the psychological inability to face the alternatives. This is the thrust of Kaufmann's charge against Plato and Aristotle. The suggestion is that we embrace this point of view not because we see that it is objectively true, but because we find it consoling and reassuring, calming our cosmological anxieties. It conforms to and reinforces our deepest fantasy, our preferred way of seeing ourselves and our metaphysical condition. By contrast, Nietzsche, having made his cultural diagnosis, calls for a toughening of the will, which is the deepest element in us, by a conscious turning away from what we find attractive and consoling, forcing ourselves to deliberately confront precisely what we find most difficult and painful. "What does not overcome me, makes me stronger," says the prophet of the *Ubermensch*, giving voice to his health-inspired vitalistic ethic, *jenseits von gut und böse*. He views the traditional, nontragic "perennial philosophy" as an example of weakening self-indulgence, reactionary backlash, and wishful thinking, masquerading as a sober and stringently objective map of the world.

In view of this attack on the motives from which have sprung the classical philosophical (not to mention the Judeo-Christian) worldview, how might tragedy function as a relevant experience and interesting challenge? Perhaps Aristotle discovered that the experience of tragedy could be enlisted and used as an opportunity to explore these doubts with an intensity and a theoretical rigor not approached or dreamt of in other areas of our experience, and thus as a way to undercut and disarm this charge of deliberate ignorance or evasion. Tragedy may indirectly uncover and provide a critically examined foundation, and thus successfully justify the claim of "science" for this new knowledge we are constructing. In this indirect approach, by confronting the diametrically opposite point of view, the experience of tragedy might be entered as a surprise supporting evidence and grounding datum for the classical, nontragic worldview in spite of the fact that, according to all appearances, it consists of a violent and unremitting *attack upon* its central thesis. Tragedy perhaps cannot supply a new intuition that will deliver a direct, causal foundation for the classical worldview, but it can take away the chief reservation that might be keeping us from embracing such, by demonstrating that, in accepting the latter, we are not necessarily fleeing compulsively from the irrationalist alternative to this vision, because we have been through it, have been able to confront it in a calm, steady, and free way, and have then—*after* the experience—come to a reasoned decision. The fact that we have been through such an experience (and both Socrates and Aristotle seem to have had a special enjoyment and preference for Euripides, whom Walter Kaufmann agrees in calling the most pessimistic of the Greek tragedians) testifies that we actually like to have our curiosity indulged concerning options we do *not* take, paths we have *not* followed—even if this examination is painful—when this is the only way we have of reassuring ourselves about the path we think is correct. More importantly, it shows that one's reaction to such a vision is not restricted to being either the immediate conversion and passionate embrace of the irrationalist alternative (that Schopenhauer, Nietzsche, Freud, and Kaufmann engage in), or the panic-filled backlash and reactionary retreat into metaphysical fantasy, which they dismiss all other responses as being. Rather, the ability to take in the tragic experience, to see it whole and to see it steady (to paraphrase and reverse Matthew Arnold), may ground a third response, one of intense but controlled attention to this prospect, coming to a reflected and free decision for or against it. After we have been through it, we have nothing more to learn from it or to be afraid of in it. Our fear of the unknown has been taken away, for the unknown has become the *known*, and it has been tragedy that has made this possible, precisely tragedy that has allowed us this special vantage point that combines intellectual clarity

with psychological security. The charge that our acceptance of the classical viewpoint is based necessarily on
fear and weakness is refuted in practice by our ability to
take in and enjoy the tragic experience itself; this is the
only kind of reassurance we may have. Anything stronger
is simply not available to us. As with Nietzsche's strategy
of producing his "most abysmal thought" (the Eternal
Recurrence of the Same), and thus a high point for civilization, the concrete *actuality* of the tragic experience
refutes the charge that we could not possibly face it.
Whatever our reaction, we remain perpetually grateful to
the playwright for having given us full access to examine,
at our leisure and to the full satisfaction of our curiosity,
an alternative cosmic viewpoint that is otherwise not
available to us, one which is a logical possibility, however, and thus merits our attention. In other words, in
tragedy Aristotle may have serendipitously stumbled
upon an experience which, far from terrifying him or
revealing his metaphysical system to be a fragile house of
cards, turned out to occasion precisely the potent kind of
thought process that became the chief and possibly the
only kind of evidence grounding and reassuring him
about his nontragic metaphysical axioms, one which in
an analogous fashion allows him to defend his philosophy as *knowledge*, although in a necessarily looser sense
of the word—the only form of knowledge possible for us
in this area. Tragedy does not challenge metaphysics to
destroy it; on the contrary, Aristotle may have discovered
that tragedy's challenge is the only way to ground it, on
the natural level, that tragedy thus makes metaphysics for
the first time respectable and complete because now its
basic theoretical axioms are justified in the only way they
can be.

Precisely because tragedy is an attack and challenge to
the classical or nontragic "perennial philosophy," Aristotle finds that it allows us a unique opportunity to examine
a point of view we are anxious about and have every right
to explore. After this experience, we are in a better posi-

tion to form our own conviction either way in a calm psychological state and balanced frame of mind ("calm of mind, all passion spent," as Milton puts it in the last line of *Sampson Agonistes*). Neither our acceptance nor our rejection need be based any longer on a knee-jerk reflex or compulsive reaction, nor is tragedy correctly or necessarily enjoyed only by those who embrace its irrationalist worldview. Tragedy can serve as a welcome tonic, a toughening challenge, and bracing counterpoint for those who esteem the world to be nontragic—and more so *after* the tragic experience than before. Tragedy removes the last and deepest reservation, and thus may serve as a potentially strengthening influence on the conviction supporting the "classical" worldview. *Contra* Kaufmann, we do not have either to capitulate *or* flee before the tragic vision. There is a third possibility, next to which the other two seem immature and precipitous. Further, the exclusive and exhaustive opposition of these two responses appears from this third point of view to be prejudicial and intolerant.

Aristotle may well have arrived at his option, as he did in other areas, by simply looking at the empirical data, that is, he went to plays. The effect that tragedy has on its audience is simply not what Plato, Nietzsche, or Kaufmann say that it is; these latter are far too rationalistic, trying to dictate to the empirical world out of their theories, rather than going to the trouble of *consulting* experience. If we actually attend the plays and observe the audience, we see that a tragedy seems to stimulate a rising, initial tension, followed by a release, and then, characteristically, not a headlong panic, but a period of quiet observation and thought. Some may not respond by embracing the tragic (irrationalist) viewpoint, but we should not conclude that this necessarily represents a cop out by that part of the audience, a failure of nerve before a vision they find too intimidating. It may, paradoxically, come directly and precisely as a result of an unflinching, powerful, and emotionally satisfying engagement with

the issues that tragedy raises. Aristotle may have discovered that tragedy can end up supplying an unexpected
psychological support for a nontragic point of view. What
he initially regarded as a questionable and perhaps suspicious diversion—and Plato regarded as a dangerous and
corrupting social menace—turns out, on closer examination, to have a curiously positive function and surprisingly relevant application within the project of
philosophy generally, and to the completion of intellectual virtue in particular. Precisely by raising the clear
prospect of the tragic (irrationalist) alternative, tragedy
can occasion an experience that provides analogical support and a surrogate grounding for the most basic (and
most speculative) assumption of the nontragic viewpoint.

Tragedy thus functions as a kind of trampoline or emotional springboard, as well as to provide surrogate evidence for the nontragic alternative. Like comedy, tragedy
indulges and exploits our desire for an alternative to the
everyday, conventional, and boring Apollonian my-
thology in which we have been drilled socially and that
we have internalized more or less uncritically since our
youth. It manipulates this boredom, engineers this irritating energy, to propel us into a previously avoided traumatic confrontation with the irrational, "unthinkable"
theology of tragedy. It may have been Aristotle's surprise
discovery that this violent employment of drama can have
a salutary effect, can be of use for occasioning the type of
dialectical reflection or intuitions (aitia) he mentions,
which may be the only way of grounding, solidifying, or
reinforcing our allegiance to the basic principles of a
nontragic contemplative science. Tragedy may function
for Aristotle in a way analogous to a well-constructed
Platonic dialogue, that is, as a series of questions and
lines of critical inquiry which operate on one another's
methods and results, so as to lead us gradually and even
without being conscious of it toward a fundamental insight concerning the subject matter at hand (which some-

times remains unstated, or is only mentioned casually).
For both Plato and Aristotle, this indirect approach may
be the only way to tie down our opinions to a cause, and
the wandering statutes of Daedalus to their pedestals, in
this speculative area of separate entities. It may be the
only way to transform our beliefs into "knowledge" in
even a looser, analogous sense. If so, this use would lift
tragedy considerably beyond the role of permissible diversion or amusement to make it a uniquely valuable, if
not absolutely essential, aid for the development of the
majority of the population, providing them a means into
the more difficult higher realms of intellectual attain-
ment. This would, in fact, explain Aristotle's soberly practical or utilitarian appreciation of tragedy in the *Politics*
quoted in the first chapter.

We are, of course, free to embrace the tragic vision as
the truth of our existence. Nietzsche and Freud do so, and
so does Kaufmann. Within this perspective and this option, we may adopt the heroic Viking stance, and like
King Lear wandering the heaths, or Ahab bellowing at the
whale, claim that, even if the universe is irrational and set
against us, we can at least still turn to face it, we can
direct our defiance back at it, rather than whimpering
away to our ignoble and worthless end. As Ahab declares
in ch. 119 of *Moby Dick:*

> Oh, thou clear spirit of clear fire, whom on these seas I as
> Persian once did worship, till in the sacramental act so
> burned by thee, that to this hour I bear the scar; I now know
> thee, thou clear spirit, and I now know thy right worship is
> defiance. To neither love nor reverence wilt thou be kind, and
> e'en for hate thou canst but kill; and all are killed. No fearless
> fool now fronts thee. I own thy speechless, placeless power;
> but to the last gasp of my earthquake life will dispute its
> unconditional, unintegral mastery in me. In the midst of the
> personified impersonal, a personality stands here. Though
> but a point at best; whenceso'er I came; whereso'er I go; yet
> while I earthly live, the queenly personality lives in me, and

feels her royal rights. But war is pain, and hate is woe. Come
in thy lowest form of love, and I will kneel and kiss thee; but
at thy highest, come as mere supernal power; and though
thou launchest navies of full-freighted worlds, there's that in
here that still remains indifferent. Oh, thou clear spirit, of thy
fire thou madest me, and like a true child of fire, I breathe it
back to thee. (Herman Melville, *Moby Dick*, New York:
Harper & Bros. Pub., 1950, pp. 547–48)

In this refusal to buckle, we may demonstrate our freedom, our capacity for nobility, excellence, and value,
which the universe wants to deny and knock from our
hands. We demonstrate this precisely by turning to face
the worst hypothesis about ourselves and the universe,
the horrible vision that may be the truth of our situation,
instead of fleeing into comfortable illusion or deliberate
ignorance, as most men do. This way, to echo Descartes's
new methodology for modern philosophy, we cannot be
deceived, no matter how powerful the "Evil Genie" may
be who is trying to deceive us. In this "preemptive strike,"
we become the "Evil Genie" to ourselves! Mixed with this
pessimism and irrationality, there can be a hidden streak
of vanity, of superiority beneath the insistence on looking
at the worst possible way things could be. Other people—
the majority of people—cannot do this. If the gods or the
cosmic powers are cruel and will destroy us, then we
resolve to at least go out "with head bloody but unbowed,"
demonstrating the strength, nobility, and freedom the universe wants to deny as a theoretical possibility. We can
turn to *know* our fate, no matter how bad or painful it is;
in *that* consists our nobility, or the display of our freedom. As Nietzsche says, by grasping the nettle firmly in
our hands without crying out and by turning to look at the
Medusa without flinching, we demonstrate our strength
and excellence, we lift ourselves up and *confer* value
upon a previously valueless existence. This is the secret
modern strategy and agenda to save freedom in a totally

rigorous, reductionistic, and deterministic landscape. In precisely this capacity and resolve to see and know the worst consists man's peculiar dignity and transcendence as well as undeniable evidence for his value and freedom in a universe that otherwise we resolve to view (and ourselves within it) as valueless and fully determined. This painful lucidity becomes a decisive piece of counterevidence, almost an act of revenge against a universe that wants to deny that we can be different or possess a value. We demonstrate our freedom by being willing and able to believe the worst about ourselves. We thereby become both prosecuting and defense attorneys in the same case in this strange attempt to save freedom by being willing to see its absence, and further, its utter impossibility. As the last word about our existence, this resolve to reduce and debunk every piece of evidence supporting freedom seems to extinguish the very possibility of freedom, but appreciated as evidence of our strength, that man may not always flee into consoling fantasy, it is intended as a whole to be entered as evidence in support of our strength, nobility, and value. This is the strange strategy and the hidden agenda behind the modern project to total scepticism and self-doubt—the "method" behind the Nietzschean madness.

If die we must, then we are resolved to die not like a dumb animal, ignorant of our fate. Rather, we will demonstrate in fact what the gods refuse to recognize or allow in theory. We will create the worst possible scenario about ourselves, and turn deliberately to face it. This irrationalist vision, this painfully achieved lucidity, becomes itself a deed, a savage act, a crucially important victory that neither the gods, the fates, nor anyone else can later take from us, by which I have salvaged a shred of freedom and value against a cosmological vision that denies both. Paradoxically, I accept this vision, and in an ingenious form of "intellectual judo," present this acceptance as a display of my nobility and strength—as indeed irrefutable evidence of my freedom. I use the weapon of my enemy to my own advantage; I use my enemy's strength to throw him for a fall. By this "intellectual judo," I demonstrate my freedom and value, paradoxically, by turning and *accepting* this vision of a malicious, irrational, unfree world as the *truth* of my existence; by the pain and difficulty involved in this maneuver, I constitute myself as a higher individual, as exceptional and valuable. I lift myself up; I *show* the strength and freedom my method itself wants to deny is possible. An actual presentation of a free act will refute all claims of its theoretical impossibility. It is a strange, perplexing, and self-opposed tactic, one made understandable by the desperation of the modern project to demonstrate human dignity and value within a philosophical discipline trained to think that progress comes only in our increased powers for scepticism, for distrusting our own constructions and solutions, and by a willingness to sustain the worst hypotheses about ourselves and our condition.[1] This program is caught in the jaws of a vice; the harder we push for a demonstration, a critical explosion of freedom and value, the harder these same critical forces push us to view this explosion sceptically, reductionistically, as only the predetermined result of natural or irrational forces. We end up fighting ourselves, in a titanic, but ultimately inconclusive struggle that will go on until death, or until we voluntarily agree to step out of it.

Such is the psychological strategy, and the heroic ethos, that has become the most popular and characteristic response to the modern philosophical dilemma, an ethos and stance given its preeminent expression in the philosophy of Nietzsche, later played out in different vocabularies by his several imitators and intellectual descendants. Kaufmann presents it as the only proper or authentic response to the experience of tragedy. It is the desperate, last-ditch hope implicit in this method, the spark of life and light stamped out repeatedly behind the method itself, that saves it from becoming total madness, as expressed in the words of the French existentialist Albert Camus in his essay on the mythological figure Sisyphus, condemned to an impossible and hence inherently futile task for all eternity:

> No one will live this fate, knowing it to be absurd, unless he does everything possible to keep before him that absurd brought to light by consciousness. . . . The lucidity that was to constitute his torture at the same time crowns his victory. There is no fate that cannot be surmounted by scorn. (A. Camus, *The Myth of Sisyphus*, New York: Knopf, 1958, 127)

This attitude, however, I submit, is not the reaction of the Greek audience to tragedy, or that of the majority of the modern audience. but rather only of those antecedently schooled in the hyper-critical ideology of late modern philosophy and determined to embrace this interpretation intransigently and to the exclusion of the possibility of counterdata. More relevantly to our own discussion is the point that Aristotle discovered, perhaps to his own surprise, that the natural and ingenuous reaction to tragedy is something different. Paradoxically, tragedy does not inculcate or proselytize on behalf of its own "tragic" or irrationalist viewpoint. It does present this point of view and insist that we take it seriously, that we consider it attentively. Aristotle discovered that the result of such attention may be the opposite of what Kaufmann and Plato expected. They have the same inauthentic and distorted view of the dynamics of tragedy, but from opposite metaphysical vantage points. Strangely, tragedy frees us to embrace the nontragic point of view, now for the first time without embarrassment or misgiving, unencumbered with anxiety that we may have failed to consider some critical reservation or important, but painful, alternative, or that we might thereby be simply fleeing a cosmic vision we find too terrible to take seriously or embrace. Whether or not that is what should happen, Aristotle reports, that is what *does* happen. Any other appreciation of the spontaneous reaction to tragedy—whether it be the Platonic or the Nietzchean—is simply inaccurate and nonempirical.

To recapitulate, Aristotle's theory is indeed deficient, but in a way Nietzsche and Kaufmann do not mention. He perhaps stopped short of giving a full explanation for the "cathartic" effect of tragedy his theory correctly identifies because it put him in mind of his philosophical sore-point, the persisting failure of his theory to account for the relations between God and the world. This deeper failure could not be corrected until Western culture experimented with expanded conventions of perfection, principally under the influence of the spreading Judeo–Christian–Islamic religions, which suggested that there could be a dynamism within God that was not an imperfection, as "motion" was for the Greeks—that there thus could be a form of perfection higher than that of being a perfect substance, having no dependencies or points of vulnerability, but rather, one following Plato's image of the sun, involving overfullness, generosity, and the desire to diffuse or communicate itself. When such an expansion is considered, we notice there are resources within Aristotle's aesthetic, ethical, rhetorical, and epistemological works to explain how tragedy might perform a useful function for the individual, not in *spite* of its scandalous and heterodox theology, but precisely *because* of this. Through an astute combination of blandishments and prods, tragedy can produce a philosophical "dark night of the soul" that appears useful as a device to lead the average person toward the higher regions of intellectual virtue and personal maturation. Specifically, this traumatic experience forces him to live vicariously through the theoretical alternative to the conventional or orthodox view in a powerfully condensed but also protected or distanced way, thereby allowing him to ground (if he so chooses) in the only way possible for us the allegiances in which he has been reared to the nontragic world view. In a way analogous to the puberty rites in many cultures, but here dealing with terrifying cosmological or metaphysical possibilities, the institution of tragedy provides an intense yet structured and sheltered occasion for this searing and transforming experience. It provides a way for the intellectual adolescent to negotiate the difficult and necessarily discontinuous transition to the adult way of being in the world, a transition in which a powerful confrontation with a terrifying experience is deliberately orchestrated, a way that shields both the individual and society, however, from the unbearable emotion and the social chaos that could otherwise result from a direct and unmediated encounter with this vision.

According to Aristotle, tragedy may not even be needed by every person, or in every life. Some people can apparently reach the highest levels of contemplative science or be induced to address the "eternal questions" without being spurred into it by the combination of seductive allurements and the irritating goad of tragedy. Still, for some these seem to be essential, and for all useful for this purpose. Thus, this cultural discovery opens the process of education or ascent to intellectual virtue to everyone, where before it was accessible only to the enlightened few—the "philosophers" or sages who could push through or ascend to this level on their own.

In contrast to the "Art for Art's Sake" ethos of the late romantic movement, tragedy is not the highest value civilization has to offer for Aristotle, but it can be a *means* to the highest value. As such, it is a singularly useful and attractive institution, if mankind is ever to move toward the higher levels of maturation and enlightenment of which it is capable. It may well be that one must live through a tragedy, either in one's own life (and learn from it directly, and perhaps at great personal cost), or vicariously through a story told about someone else, thus saving oneself the personal pain, to advance to this level. Tragedy appears as a condensed, economic, and efficient way of achieving the latter. Tragedy gives us the option of inoculating ourselves with a weakened form of the bacillus by this artificial experience, one to which, however, our psyches may respond in a way analogous to the disease itself. The nobility of poetry, as Wallace Stevens says, is "a violence from within that protects us from a violence without." In this sense, perhaps, tragedy was essential or required for the social or cultural development of philosophy (as opposed to individual or private enlightenment), for the speculative metaphysical systems of Plato and Aristotle, and for what came afterwards during the Middle Ages. In that sense, perhaps tragedy helped to give rise to philosophy.

Like comedy, tragedy seems peculiarly suited and crafted to meet our creaturely needs; like comedy, but now in the theoretical order, it seems to acknowledge our metaphysical weakness, our desire for variety and yet to know the real, but also our inability to pierce through to the highest and most important speculative assumptions. Tragedy in this sense seems to run forward and accommodate itself to our condition, a "grace" sent to meet our "nature," to take account of both our desire and our limitations. By a clever engineering of our restlessness and our lower desires, it manages to lift us up to where we cannot otherwise easily go. It appears a form of god's mercy towards us—the Aristotelian god, who in this regard may not be as aloof or uncaring as he is at first depicted. Aristotle was wrestling with this tension in his philosophy; he may have lived through to a better dispensation than he imagined. Tragedy seems not a luxury, but a necessity if we are to reach the higher stages of our projected development. It is a crutch God appears to have given us, in view of our limping condition and limited ability to meet our own needs, cultural as well as psychological, and of our unrealistically high aspirations for self-fulfillment (which he may have planted in us—so in a sense he is beholden); a compensation he gives us through civilization to make up for what he could not give us through nature. Indeed, the two genres seem to have an almost magical, preordained or superhuman origin; they complete us, or send us off, in an Aristotelian perspective, toward our completion as nothing else in the natural or social realm can, and without which we appear to remain half-finished. The two together constitute a secular sacrament, bringing about something close to a "substantial change" in us the first time we receive them, and yet allowing us to feed repeatedly on them afterward without becoming exhausted. Nothing else in the natural world does that. Tragedy allows us to reassure ourselves concerning paths and options we have not taken, to ground our beliefs and to transform them into knowledge insofar as this is possible for us, and it allows us to generate the energy needed to propel ourselves into those higher reaches of contemplative knowledge and intellectual virtue where the pleasures, which perhaps only gods enjoy in their purity and fullness, wait to meet and cheer us.

Notes

Introduction

1. Actually, this romantic and postromantic group of thinkers was much more under the influence of Schopenhauer's and Nietzsche's general *Weltanschauung* than is generally recognized. They regard tragedy, for instance, as one of the signal achievements of Western civilization, but have a difficult time explaining precisely in what its greatness consists. When they do succeed, their descriptions tend to fall into Nietzschean terms and criteria. Edith Hamilton is quite representative when she writes:

> Only twice in literary history has there been a great period of tragedy, in the Athens of Pericles and in Elizabethan England. What these two periods had in common . . . may give us some hint of the nature of tragedy, for far from being periods of darkness and defeat, each was a time when life was seen exalted, a time of thrilling and unfathomable possibilities. They held their heads high, those men who conquered at Marathon and Salamis, and those who fought Spain and saw the Great Armada sink. The world was a place of wonder; mankind was beauteous; life was lived on the crest of the wave. (Edith Hamilton, *The Greek Way* (New York: W. W. Norton & Co., 1958, 232)

Miss Hamilton regards the ability to write tragedies as a measure of the "greatness" of a civilization, appreciated in health-inspired, vitalistic, or power-quantum categories (i.e., the ability to write tragedies may be used as a criterion to separate "strong" from "weak" cultures). Presumably, what makes tragedy so important and culturally indicative is that it allows us (and demands of us the strength) to come close to and view steadily the irrational core of the universe, or the worst about ourselves. Again, this is Schopenhauer's and Nietzsche's appreciation of tragedy.

2. For a fuller account of the internal inadequacy within the Aristotelian system than is given here, see my *Christian Revelation and the Completion of the Aristotelian Revolution,* University Press of America, Lanham, MD., 1988, chs. 1 and 2.

3. Walter Kaufmann, *Tragedy and Philosophy* (Princeton, N.J.: Princeton University Press, 1979), 48, 59. Hereafter "T&P."

Chapter 1. The Contemporary Attack

1. Paul Ricoeur, *The Symbolism of Evil*, trans. Buchanan, (Boston: Beacon Press, 1969), 350–57. Hereafter "SE."

2 Gerald Graff, *Literature against Itself* (Chicago: The University of Chicago Press, 1979).

3. See Ricoeur: "The non-distinction between the divine and the diabolical is the implicit theme of the tragic theology and anthropology. Perhaps . . . it was this non-distinction that could not be *thought through* right to the end and that caused the downfall of tragedy and its vehement condemnation by philosophy in the second book of the *Republic*. But if the feeling that good and evil are identical in God resists thought, it is projected in dramatic works that give rise to indirect, but nevertheless troubling, reflection" (SE, 214).

4. Kaufmann, T&P, 287–300.

Chapter 3. Comedy and Moral Virtue

1. Henri Bergson, in his famous essay on laughter, explores the degree to which comedy is the means by which society brings the "eccentric" individual back into line with the social norm. See *Laughter; An Essay on the Meaning of the Comic*, in *Comedy*, by George Meredith, Garden City, N.Y.: Doubleday, 1956.

2. We notice that the structure of this comic plot is similar to the "sophisticated" tragic plot (where the hero recognizes the truth in time to prevent major suffering) that Aristotle prefers. In both, suffering to the hero and the audience is toned down or minimized compared to what it could have been, and yet an experience is produced that occasions the audience's moving toward a nontragic metaphysic (tragedy) or social outlook (comedy). Thus, in both, an "optimistic" theology is salvaged, safeguarded, and sustained. Perhaps then tragedy is also "practical" or "utilitarian" in function, in an analogous sense to comedy, in the sense of allowing us to deal with our periodic rebellious tendencies against the theological or theoretic "orthodoxy," the benign interpretation of the gods, and producing an experience that allows us to return, affectively as well as intellectually, and to be reconciled to this staid, received, and routine view.

3. "The Whiffenpoof Song" by T. B. Galloway, M. Hart, M. Minnigerode, G. S. Pomeroy, and R. Vallee. Copyright © 1936, 1944 (renewed 1964, 1972) Miller Music Corporation. Rights assigned to EMI Catalogue Partnership. All rights controlled and administered by EMI Miller Catalog Inc. International copyright secured. All rights reserved.

4. The power of art to blur the demarcation between reality and make-believe, and to trigger our uninhibited, spontaneous emotions, is at the base of Hamlet's strategy against his uncle:

I have heard
That guilty creatures, sitting at a play,

> Have by the very cunning of the scene
> Been struck so to the soul that presently
> They have proclaimed their malefactions.
>
> (act 2, sc. 2)

Chapter 4. Raising the Pucker Factor

1. One of the most sensitive and insightful appreciations of the Book of Job is given by Gerhard Von Rad in his classic *Wisdom in Israel* (Nashville, Tenn.: Abingdon Press, 1972). Although allowing for a resolution in a sense (223–26), Von Rad notes that "[the poet] lets the men unfold their positions and lets the dialogue end without a conclusion. Indeed, at the end the disagreement is greater than it was at the beginning. Only in the fact that the poet allows Job to reply to each speech of the friends and therefore lets him speak more frequently, lies an indication of where the centre of gravity of the dialogue lies" (215–6). In the prologue, Job amazingly maintains an unshakeable faith in God in spite of his great suffering, thus allowing God to "win" his wager with Satan. In this traditional part of the story, "in a moment of the greatest importance, (Job) has clearly taken up a position with regard to something that was of concern to God. To utter anything 'unseemly' about God would be something to be detested. It was a duty, in a critical situation, to say the 'right' thing about God" (208). Into this edifying folktale a large literary block of dialogue was inserted, probably centuries later. Von Rad finds "something completely new and unique has emerged by means of a certain shift of emphasis or of a radicalization of traditional forms of speech" (209). Here Job achieves "a much more grandiose outburst. . . . Can we call what Job did anything else but resentment?" (210). Specifically,

[I]f one seeks to distinguish the main thought from the stream of laments, reproaches, protestations and abuse which he hurls at his friends in turn or directly at God, one will need to mention the three following groups of thoughts. Job feels that he is in the right with regard to God and continues to protest his innocence. By this he means that he feels himself unable to admit in his own case the correspondence which is asserted by the friends between guilt and punishment. He cannot admit that the breach in his relationship with God has emanated from him, that is, from some heinous sin on his part. . . . [Secondarily], [h]e must achieve a discussion between himself and God. . . . But [thirdly], Job is still not able to find peace in this conviction. On a much broader basis there appears in his laments the argument that it is hopeless and impossible to expect justice from this God. He will not even listen to his arguments, far less answer them. God is so free that he establishes his own justice and does not bother about what men think justice is." (213–15)

Von Rad concludes: "No one in Israel had ever depicted the action of God towards men in this way before: . . . God as the direct enemy of men, delighting in torturing them, hovering over them like what we might call the caricature of a devil, gnashing his teeth, 'sharpening' his eyes . . . and splitting open Job's intestines. One cannot but affirm that Job stands face to face with a completely new experience of the reality of God, an experience of something incalculable and fearful, . . . faced with which Job's friends were utterly helpless" (217). The reversal of ethical stance from the traditional story is now almost complete: "[Job's] conviction that he is free of all blame is almost disconcerting in the way in which it remains unshakeable. 'Who is there that will contend with me?' (13.9)" (219). For a more recent analysis of *Job* along similar lines, see David Noel Freedman, "Is It Possible to Understand the Book of Job?", *Bible Review*, vol. IV, no. 2 (April 1988): 26–34.

Chapter 5. The Surprise Effect

1. For a fuller account of this distinctive modern project to overcome scepticism by *increasing* scepticism, and ultimately to defend the reality of freedom by embracing a deterministic fatalism, see my *The Modern Project to Rigor; Descartes to Nietzsche* (Lanham, Md.: University Press of America, 1986).

Select Bibliography

In his *Tragedy and Philosophy* (Princeton: Princeton University Press, 1979), Walter Kaufmann gives an extensive bibliography on the discussion of these topics through 1966 that should serve the reader as a powerful instrument with which to begin various researches. In addition, the following works may be consulted.

Albrecht, W. P. *The Sublime Pleasures of Tragedy: A Study of Critical Theory from Dennis to Keats.* Lawrence, Kans.: University Press of Kansas, 1975.

Barbour, John D. *Tragedy as a Critique of Virtue: The Novel and Ethical Reflection.* Georgia: Scholars Press, 1984.

Belsey, Catherine. *The Subject of Tragedy.* New York: Routledge Chapman & Hall, 1985.

Berlin, Normand. *The Secret Cause: A Discussion of Tragedy.* Amherst, Mass.: University of Massachusetts Press, 1983.

Brashear, William R. *The Gorgon's Head: A Study in Tragedy and Despair.* Athens, Ga.: University of Georgia Press, 1977.

Brereton, Geoffrey. *Principles of Tragedy: A Rational Examination of the Tragic Concept in Life and Literature.* Baltimore, Md.: University of Miami Press, 1968.

Evans, J. D. G. *Aristotle's Concept of Dialectic.* New York: Cambridge University Press, 1977.

Faas, Ekbert. *Tragedy and After: Euripides, Shakespeare, and Goethe.* Cheektowaga, N.Y.: McGill-Queens University Press, 1984.

Green, Andre. *The Tragic Effect.* New York: Cambridge University Press, 1979.

Janko, Richard. *Aristotle on Comedy: Towards a Reconstruction of Poetics II.* Berkeley, Calif.: University of California Press, 1984.

Jepsen, Laura. *Ethical Aspects of Tragedy.* Lawrence, Kans.: AMS Press, 1953.

Mandel, Oscar. *A Definition of Tragedy.* Lanham, Md.: University Press of America, 1982.

Nussbaum, Martha C. *The Fragility of Goodness: Luck and Ethics in Greek Tragedy and Philosophy.* New York: Cambridge University Press, 1986.

Sewall, Richard B. *The Vision of Tragedy.* New Haven, Conn.: Yale University Press, 1979.

Silk, S. M. and J. P. Stern. *Nietzsche on Tragedy.* New York: Cambridge University Press, 1983.

Trimpi, Wesley. *Muses of One Mind; The Literary Analysis of Experience and Its Continuity.* Princeton, N.J.: Princeton University Press, 1983.

Von Rad, Gerhard. *Wisdom in Israel.* Nashville, Tenn.: Abingdon Press, 1978.

Index